Desmond's Guide
to
Perfect Entertaining

By the same authors:

That Girl and Phil
At Your Service

DESMOND'S GUIDE TO

Perfect Entertaining

Desmond Atholl

&

Michael Cherkinian

ST. MARTIN'S PRESS
NEW YORK

DESIGN BY JAYE ZIMET

Library of Congress Cataloging-in-Publication Data

Atholl, Desmond.
    Desmond's guide to perfect entertaining / Desmond Atholl and Michael Cherkinian.
        p. cm.
    "A Thomas Dunne book."
    ISBN 0-312-09921-5
    1. Entertaining. I. Cherkinian, Michael. II. Title.
III. Title: Guide to perfect entertaining.
TX731.A79   1993
642'.4—dc20   93-25681
                                                      CIP

First Edition: November 1993

10 9 8 7 6 5 4 3 2 1

Contents

Acknowledgments

The authors would like to express their gratitude to the following individuals for their assistance: Reagan Arthur, Doris Borowsky-Straus, Tom Dunne, Benno Friedman, Jacki Gelb, Toni Lopopolo, Barbara Lowenstein, Eric Meyer, Laura Mullen, Claudia Riemer, Dr. Barry Rosenthal, Nancy Yost, Joann Reardon, and the gracious employees of Pierre Deaux who helped us create the perfect cover for *Perfect Entertaining*.

Acknowledgments

Introduction

Although there are hundreds of books available on the general topic of "entertaining," few focus on the plans, procedures, and problems involved whenever you

> **"Fantastic food alone does not a dazzling dinner party make!"**
> —Desmond Atholl

extend an invitation. Most of the publications I have examined are either cookbooks, offering an assortment of elaborate recipes, or coffee table tomes, filled with pretty pictures of flowers and food. Although these volumes are excellent resources for new cooking ideas and can provide many pleasurable hours of "paging through the pictures," they rarely answer a host's inevitable list of practical questions, such as:

1. *What do you do if a guest has an accident in your home?*

2. *How do you prepare a budget for a dinner party?*

3. *How do you handle inebriated guests?*

4. *What can you do if you're tired but one of the guests will not leave?*

5. *How can you politely implement a "No-Smoking" policy?*

6. *What is the proper way to set a table?*

7. *What do you do if an unexpected guest arrives for a seated dinner party?*

8. *Is it possible to purchase a bottle of wine without feeling intimidated?*

Entertaining has always been an important part of my life. If adolescence is the prologue to the book of one's life then my childhood certainly set the stage for the dynamic dramas of my career. At an age when most children learn to read, I began planning make-believe celebrations for my collection of stuffed animals, period costume balls for a pair of peculiar aunts, and Broadway-styled extravaganzas for my sister's birthdays—all of which prepared me for my future career as a first-class, fast paced, globe-trotting majordomo.

Growing up in a fifty-five room Georgian manor which was colored by the mix of a strict Victorian Englishman (my grandfather) and an eccentric but fun-loving ex-actress (my grandmother) influenced the approach I would take to my personal and professional lives. I learned to combine organization and discipline with a sense of fun and adventure; an approach that characterizes my idea of "perfect entertaining." Throughout my career people have called me a "walking encyclopedia of unique information"; employers often remarked that not only did I organize a perfect party but I appeared to be having a tremendous amount of fun in the process. Many of them suggested that I should outline my methods on paper; guests whom I have entertained in my home frequently concurred.

Desmond's Guide to Perfect Entertaining offers comprehensive advice for party-planning. Each chapter outlines my approach to a particular subject; the suggestions are illustrated with examples and anecdotes from my experiences. Defining your own entertaining style, however, is not based on selecting a *particular* method (even mine) but is derived from *combining* and *adapting* everything you read and experience. Do not implement ideas or suggestions that do not make sense to you, or do not suit your lifestyle.

Making comfortable choices is the key to all successful entertaining.

Accidents

A host or hostess's primary responsibility is to create an atmosphere in which a guest can relax—no matter *what* happens. It's inevitable: at some point, you will have an accident in someone's home and look into your host's face for redemption. A good host should provide you with social salvation as quickly and quietly as possible. Unless your objective is to shorten your future guest lists be prepared for accidents: define an approach for managing mishaps.

◆ The 5 steps for handling accidents

Take Positive Control of the Situation Immediately • Approximately three seconds after an accident occurs the focus of the room will shift from the broken item (and the embarrassed guest who created the situation) to you (the host). A failure to act quickly and positively resolve the crisis will keep your guests from relaxing.

Many years ago, I attended a cocktail party in Los Angeles given by an aging Hollywood agent. The once super-saleswoman of the stars wanted to share the magnificence of her recently redecorated Bel Air mansion. One hour into the party a high-spirited Hollywood Hopeful tripped on her four-inch heels, emptying a glass of red wine onto a cream couch. No one moved; no one spoke. It was as if someone had pressed the "pause" button on the VCR. One hundred pairs of eyes quickly scanned the room until they locked in on their target. The moment our hostess saw the soiled sofa she froze. As the seconds ticked by she continued her impersonation of a tortured figure in a wax museum. When the now Hollywood Hopeless tried to apologize for her clumsy behavior the hostess's fringed mu-mu began to quiver with such ferocity that she resembled a deranged hula dancer. The instant the performance reached its climax the agitated agent released the kind of scream usually associated with childbirth. Most of the guests departed immediately thereafter. This behavior exemplifies taking *negative* control of a situation.

Determine to What Extent Your Guest Has Been Hurt—Both Physically and Emotionally • Focus on the physical condition of the individual—not the broken object. If a guest cracks a glass, knocks over a vase or trips on the carpet, make sure he (or she) is not cut, scraped or bruised. The *emotional* well-being of the embarrassed individual will also require careful attention. A skilled host or hostess is one who alleviates that embarrassment as quickly as possible.

When I was entertaining a group of friends in Los Angeles, Eleanor, an elderly friend of my mother's, lost her balance upon rising from the sofa. She toppled onto the glass coffee table, cracking it in two. Miraculously she wasn't hurt. But when Eleanor saw what had happened she began crying uncontrollably. After assisting her

back onto the sofa, I told my embarrassed guest that I had been agonizing for months over whether to replace the table—"I never liked it." I convinced her that the accident was a blessing in disguise that had resolved my decision-making crisis. I further assured her that nothing could be more valuable than the safety and well-being of a visitor in my home. With the help of a few kind words (and a shot of brandy) Eleanor stopped crying and the party continued as if the accident had never occurred.

Clean the Mess as Quickly as Possible to Ensure That No One Else Will Become Injured • Cleaning the broken item as quickly as possible will not only ensure the safety of your other guests but it will remove a symbol which might otherwise dampen the party spirit. In Eleanor's case, I asked two of my friends to replace the broken object with a small marble table from another room. I felt it was important to replace the cracked item so it wouldn't continually remind everyone (especially Eleanor) of the accident.

Think Quickly and Don't Panic • When I was working in Los Angeles for a rock star I organized a lavish pool-side buffet. Ninety minutes before the guests were scheduled to arrive a gust of wind buckled the leg of the buffet table. In less than ten seconds $12,000 worth of lobster, shrimp and chicken teriyaki slid into the Olympic-sized pool. The household staff began to scream; the caterer cried. I took a deep breath and did the only sensible thing: I pressed the button which released the marble cover over the pool. Within minutes the ghastly gastronomic sight was erased. I then placed an emergency call to the caterer's headquarters and requested new supplies. We had an "extended" cocktail hour until the extra food arrived; I cleaned the contents of the pool the next day. When the rock star asked why the pool had been covered I explained it was for the safety of his guests.

Use Humor to Break the Tension • Accidents create tension that can alter the mood of a party. Once you have dealt with the individual who had the accident and removed all physical traces of the crisis, alleviate the tension by recounting amusing anecdotes of similar experiences. If someone knocks over a glass remind them about the time you tripped into the three-tiered cake at your cousin's wedding. If your sister-in-law drops a roasted potato on the carpet tell her about the evening you were served unripened cantaloupe for desert and accidentally shot a melon ball into the hostess's eye. These stories will remind your guests that accidents can happen to anyone.

◆ Accident prevention tips

Although there is little you can do to ensure accidents *never* occur, certain measures can minimize the potential for mishaps.

1. No matter how many times you say "it doesn't matter" when an accident occurs, if it *does* matter your guests will notice. If you're the type of person who is traumatized by breakages, don't use family heirlooms or valuable china and glassware. Whenever possible, put your prized possessions away.

2. Make practical food and beverage choices for specific events. If you have wall-to-wall white carpeting and you're organizing a graduation party for your son's twenty-five college friends, don't plan an indoor Mexican buffet with sangria.

3. Don't invite more people than your home can comfortably accommodate.

4. Don't create or encourage an atmosphere where you might lose control of the event.

5. Always monitor the alcohol level of your guests.

6. When entertaining couples with children, remove breakable items; don't use your most expensive china and glassware.

7. Whenever possible, purchase the type of home insurance that will cover accidents.

Ralph Waldo Emerson once said, "The ornaments of a house are the friends who frequent it." I can think of no quicker way to shatter a valued ornament than by making a guest feel bad for something he never intended to do.

Bars & Bartenders

Sharing a drink with a friend or acquaintance in the intimacy of your home is a wonderful way to relax. The opportunity to let down one's guard and talk freely in a private home—instead of a public bar or restaurant—can be more rejuvenating than two hours of therapy with a trained analyst.

The type, variety and amount of alcohol you choose to serve will

> "Then trust me,
> there's nothing
> like drinking
> So pleasant on this
> side the grave;
> It keeps the
> unhappy from
> thinking,
> And makes even the
> valiant more
> brave.
>
> **—Charles Dibdin
> (1745–1814)**

vary based upon individual preferences and attitudes about drinking. As a true believer in the social powers of champagne, I serve the effervescent elixir whenever I entertain (see "Champagne"). I have organized many parties, however, for a variety of employers who offered a selection of every type of drink imaginable.

The following lists and suggestions will assist you in stocking a bar, setting it up for a party and deciding who, if anyone, should "play bartender."

◆ Stocking the bar

Unless you entertain on a weekly basis, I recommend purchasing liquor twice a year. Make a master list of what you will need in the months to come; buy everything from large stores that advertise discounted prices. You'll save time, money, and the aggravation which comes from visiting overcrowded shops during such popular holiday times as Christmas and New Year's Eve. Size of bottles and quantities should be based on your entertaining habits. If possible, keep a log of your purchases to help you plan for your next big "shop." If you are unsure about specific brands or require recommendations, ask a salesperson for assistance.

ALCOHOLIC SUPPLIES

Liquor • Unless I know I will be organizing a very large party, I buy single liter sizes of the following liquors: vodka (which should be stored in the freezer), gin, scotch, whiskey, rum and vermouth. For very large parties (over 100) gallon-size bottles are economical.

Wine, Beer and Champagne • If you have adequate storage facilities, purchase wine, beer and champagne by the case. For more specific information, see "Wine" and "Champagne."

Liqueurs • Offering a selection of liqueurs with coffee after dinner is the perfect way to conclude a fine meal. Stock at least two or three of the following types: Cointreau, Sambuca, Grand Marnier, Frangelico, Kahlua, Brandy, Cognac, Benedictine, or Amaretto.

NON-ALCOHOLIC SUPPLIES

Mixers • For mixed drinks you'll need: tonic water, seltzer, ginger ale and soda water.

Juices • You should also have on hand: orange, grapefruit, cranberry and tomato juice.

Assorted Soft Drinks • With choices including sugar-full, sugar-free, caffeinated, non-caffeinated, dark colas, clear colas and "un-colas," trying to offer a comprehensive selection of soft drinks requires multiple refrigerators. I recommend narrowing the field to two types of soft drinks in addition to a bottled sparkling water such as Perrier or San Pellegrino.

Glasses • A well-stocked bar should have a variety of glasses, including: champagne, wine, beer, collins, whiskey tumblers (sometimes called "highball glasses"), liqueur, and brandy snifters. For very large parties I recommend plastic glasses, which simplify the cleaning process and safeguard against the dangers of broken glass.

Garnishes • "A drink always looks better if it's well-dressed." Keep a supply of: oranges, cherries, lemons, limes, olives, celery and cocktail onions.

Miscellaneous Supplies • A bar worth its name should include: toothpicks, swizzle sticks, cocktail napkins, two bottle openers, a can opener, corkscrew, ice, straws, ice buckets or chests, a cocktail shaker, a blender (optional) and a trash bin.

◆ Setting up the bar

If you're setting up a full bar, try and do it the day before your party. Slice the necessary oranges, lemons, and limes, and store them in a Tupperware container in the refrigerator. Organize glasses by size and liquor by variety. Make sure everything is clearly visible and within an arm's reach. Depending upon the size of the party you may want to set up more than one bar to better serve your guests. I recommend the use of movable trolleys, which can be relocated and restocked with a minimum amount of fuss. Unless you have a location in your home that is the designated bar area, organize the supplies on a small table in a clutter-free corner of the entertaining space. Crowds frequently congregate around the bar; setting it up in a small space will frustrate your guests and may present a safety hazard. If necessary, rearrange the furniture to allow ample "lingering" room while the guests are waiting for their drinks.

◆ Bartenders

Selecting someone to "play bartender" at your party requires careful consideration. The individual must be (a) knowledgeable about how to prepare, garnish and serve a variety of drinks, (b) efficient enough to handle a thirsty crowd without becoming anxious, (c) socially entertaining to engage in casual conversation, and (d) responsible enough to monitor the guests' levels of alcohol consumption. Consider the following options before making a choice:

Do It Yourself • Unless the group is very small (6–8) or you're only serving wine and champagne I rarely recommend that the host act as bartender. With the endless lists of entertaining details to occupy your thoughts, the last thing you need to worry about is "How do you make a Manhattan?" or "What is the correct garnish for a Martini?"

Spouses, Friends or Relatives • Spouses, friends and relatives are the most popular and practical choice for a bartender. Most families or groups of friends have one person who loves to mix the drinks and open the wine. And using the services of someone you trust will alleviate any worries you might have when hiring a stranger.

Hired Help • If you don't have any friends or relatives you can call upon, hire someone. An understaffed bar area creates agitated and unhappy guests who will either (a) depart early, or (b) take it out on the already frazzled bartender. Caterers or special temporary employment agencies that feature party-helpers can provide you with assistance (usually for $10–15 an hour plus tip with a four-hour minimum).

If you hire bartenders be very specific about such topics as: monitoring alcohol consumption; how to handle a problematic situation; how strong and how tall to pour the drinks; breaks. Be as clear as possible before the evening begins to prevent any uncomfortable situations during the party itself.

Self-Service Bar • Except for very small groups (4 people or less), I rarely recommend this as an option. Without someone acting as bartender, the bar area becomes messy and disorganized, and no one can monitor the guests' alcohol consumption.

No matter what type of alcohol you serve or whom you select to pour the drinks, always remember that one of your fundamental responsibilities as host is to safeguard the well being of your guests—especially when that well being is affected by alcohol consumption. Better to risk temporarily offending a friend by limiting their intake than losing them forever through an unfortunate accident. As the saying goes, "Friends don't let friends drive drunk."

Bathrooms

Have you ever tried a new restaurant but waited to inspect the bathrooms before offering a critique? There is nothing more disappointing (in either a restaurant or a home) than to have a perfect dining experience diminished by an untidy and neglected bathroom. Because they are such "private places," hosts may forget to inspect guest bathrooms. The time and attention invested in the presentation of this particular room, however, should be equal to any other entertaining space in your home. Necessary supplies must be stocked; the floors and counter tops should be immaculate. I recommend using the following checklist for preparing a bathroom whenever you are expecting guests.

◆ **Bathroom checklist**

1. Make sure all surfaces (including the floor, sink, counter tops, tub, and toilet) are spotlessly clean.
2. Clean all mirrored and chrome surfaces, and check for water spots and finger prints.
3. Set out guest towels (either cloth or a high-quality paper) in a manner which indicates "use these." It is frustrating and embarrassing to find yourself standing in a strange bathroom with dripping hands, trying to decide if you're sup-

pose to use the picture-perfect Porthault towels hanging on the side wall or the paper napkins resting on the bathtub. I use white paper towels, carefully stacked in a white ceramic container next to the sink.

4. Set out a clean, empty bin for used paper towels and tissues. I always line my bins with small white plastic garbage bags to simplify the cleaning process. Make sure the bin is visible—not placed inside the vanity or completely hidden under the commode.

5. Replace the existing roll of toilet paper with a new roll. Make sure there are additional supplies in one of the bathroom cabinets or the vanity.

6. Keep a full tissue container in a visible location.

7. Place either a bar of soap or a selection of small guest soaps in a decorative soap dish.

8. Empty the cabinets of any personal items you may not want particularly inquisitive guests to uncover. It is a strange but well-known quirk of human nature that certain guests have an irresistible urge to go poking into places which should, otherwise, remain private. Be prepared for inquiring minds.

◆ **Additional items of consideration**

The following items, while not essential, are a welcome addition to any guest bathroom.

1. A matched comb, brush and hand mirror on the vanity counter.

2. A small selection of perfumes and colognes—

the sample sizes given away for promotional purposes are perfect.

3. An assortment of breath sprays placed in a ceramic cup.

4. A scented candle or incense.

5. Flowers: a single rose in a bud vase or a small arrangement of silk flowers dresses up any bathroom.

◆ **Spot checks**

Periodically (once an hour) check the guest bathroom(s) during the party to ensure that everything is in order. If there are tissues carelessly tossed on the floor or water splashed across the sink, quickly tidy the room. Spot checking will simplify the cleaning up process. (See "Cleaning Up.")

Budgets perform two very important functions:

1. They help to establish a financial plan of attack; *and*

2. They ensure the emotional and financial stability *of your relationship with your loved one and/or yourself.*

Throughout my career as a majordomo I have organized an assortment of soirées for a collection of rich and royal personalities. Although the majority of my employers never concerned themselves with those unpleasant "B" words ("budgets and bills"), some became quite vociferous whenever I presented a folder containing the receipts from a particular event. These outspoken employers could never understand how *I* had spent so much for a *single* occasion. I always reminded them that the party occurred in *their* home and for *their* friends; they had dictated a standard and, in almost all instances, had pre-approved my choices.

People frequently want "the best" but are rarely willing to quietly assume the financial responsibility. Affluent individuals often mistake "the most expensive" for "the best." But excessive spending is not a prerequisite for successful entertaining. If you overspend for a particular event and feel angry afterwards, the memory of the occasion is tarnished. Outline and adhere to a strict budget, and you won't regret or dread entertaining.

◆ Developing a budget

To develope an entertainment budget, answer two important questions:

1. How much do I wish to spend (if you have unlimited resources) or how much can I afford to spend for the entire event?

2. How do I want to divide that amount between the various entertaining expenditures (food, beverages, alcohol, flowers, centerpieces, table gifts, etc.)?

Once you have decided upon an overall budget, divide that amount into the following three categories:

Food ● (Approximately half of the budget.) This includes everything from appetizers to the main course and dessert. Unless you're a wine enthusiast who feels compelled to serve an '82 Chateaux Margeaux at every dinner party, food will be your largest expenditure. Because dinner parties are, by definition, focused on food, I recommend allocating half of the budget for groceries.

Beverages ● (Approximately a quarter of the budget.) The beverage budget includes only soft drinks, beer, wine and champagne. If you eliminate alcohol from a particular event, incorporate the savings into your other entertaining expenditures.

Flowers, Centerpieces, Table Gifts, etc •
(Approximately a quarter of the budget.) This category has the greatest flexibility and can include: fresh flowers, centerpieces, placecards, table gifts, invitations, music, and any miscellaneous expenditures.

◆ **Sample budgets**

The following examples offer two very different budgets for two very different occasions, using the formula outlined above.

$60 BUDGET FOR A CASUAL DINNER FOR 4

Food ($30)

Appetizer:	pita with hummus (chick pea dip) ($5)
Main Course:	salad, grilled lemon chicken breasts with carrots and green beans ($20)
Dessert:	raspberry sorbet ($5)

Drink ($15)

Wine:	2 bottles of Beaujolais Nouveau

Flowers, etc ($15)

Flowers:	white tulips ($6)

Table Gift:	Two 4-piece boxes of inexpensive chocolates ($3)
Substitution:	Use the extra $6 savings to buy an inexpensive bottle of champagne to serve either before or after dinner

$200 BUDGET FOR AN ANNIVERSARY DINNER FOR 4

Food ($100)

Appetizer:	shrimp cocktail ($25)
Main Course:	salad, grilled tuna with baby vegetables ($55)
Dessert:	individual fruit tarts ($20)

Drink ($50)

Champagne:	1 bottle of Chandon
Wine:	2 bottles of Pouilly Fuissé

Flowers, etc. ($50)

Flowers:	fresh flowers ($15)
Centerpiece:	$15
Table Gift:	2 4-piece boxes of Godiva chocolates ($10)
Placecards:	photo cards of the anniversary couple ($10)

Think of budgeting as a creative exercise rather than a form of punishment. I've enjoyed the challenge of a $30 luncheon for 4 as much as a million dollar dinner-dance for 400. It's not the amount of money you invest in a particular occasion but the time, thought and creativity that make it a success.

Cancellations & No-Shows

Overcoming the obstacles of last-minute cancellations and no-shows is like cooking with substitutions: mix a dash of imagination with a of pinch of adventure and the end result can be surprisingly pleasant. Everyone has experienced that nerve-wracking, heart-pounding moment when the telephone rings twenty-five minutes before the guests are scheduled to arrive. You pick up the receiver as if it were made of egg shells, dreading the information you know you are about to receive. Is it the lady or the tiger? A harmless wrong number, or the affirmation of all your worst fears. Two minutes later, gasping for air, the telephone slips from your trembling hand. Balancing yourself between the counter top and the carpet you realize that a perfectly planned sit-down dinner for six has been reduced to a frantically reorganized feast for four. You dial "911" requesting emergency medical assistance seconds before you pass out. The presence of the paramedics provides the perfect excuse for canceling the entire affair and taking to your bed.

On the other hand, a last-minute cancellation is infinitely preferable—and for more polite—than an out-and-out no-show. Whenever I extend invitations to potential guests I always inform them of the size and nature of the particular event: a sit-down dinner for six; a holiday cocktail party for twenty-five; a champagne and dessert reception for forty. Such information not only helps the guests decide whether to eat before attending and what to wear but it also lets them know to what extent their absence would be missed if, for any reason, they were unable to attend. There is an enormous difference between not arriving for a large cocktail party and a formal sit-down dinner. It is an extreme act of rudeness to place the host in dinner-party-purgatory, not knowing whether a guest is lost, running late, dead, or worse: a "no-show."

◆ **How to handle cancellations**

Thank the Guest for Telephoning • Having once cancelled at the last minute myself I understand it requires a bit of courage and demonstrates a degree of courtesy to telephone a host moments before the designated arrival time and apologetically state that you are about to ruin the evening. Such courage should be acknowledged with a proper "thank-you for telephoning."

Assure the Guest That You "Understand" • Whatever excuse your canceling guest offers, tell him (or her) that you "understand completely"—even if you don't. If the canceling individual is well-mannered enough to telephone chances are that he has a conscience and will want to be absolved of all social sins. Imagine yourself the father confessor with the power to exonerate a "sinner in the hands of an angry host." Absolve the penitential person with as much understanding as you can muster.

Assure the Guest You Will Invite Him or Her Again • Tell your caller that you look forward to seeing him soon; he will be at the top of your party list in the weeks to come. This will *convince* the guest that you really do understand.

Examine the Situation from the Canceling Guest's Perspective • Instead of focusing on how you have been inconvenienced, make the effort to understand why the guest had to cancel. Remember that sometimes people have to cancel for reasons beyond their control.

Replacements? • If you decide to replace the canceling guest make a list of potential candidates who (a) would mix with guest list, (b) would not be offended by the last-minute invite, and (c) live nearby. Don't be embarrassed about issuing an "eleventh hour" invitation. If you explain the situation, most people will understand. I have a handful of friends who have assisted me on numerous occasions; they understand the circumstances and are always willing to fill out a dinner table. Neighbors (because they live nearby) and relatives (because they are bound to you for life) often make good substitutes. Do not issue last-minute invitations to guests whom you do not entertain on a regular basis.

Reset the Table • If you are replacing guests and using placecards don't forget to change the names on the cards. If you aren't making a substitution for the canceling guest remove the additional place setting and adjust the table accordingly.

Stay Calm • Be flexible. If you allow the cancellation to disturb you it will color the evening. I often have last-minute cancellations which, no matter how traumatic they may seem at the time, result in a wonderfully entertaining evening.

◆ Sample Scenarios

The next paragraph lists three common excuses offered by canceling guests. The explanations are followed by "wrong" and "right" responses.

CANCELLATION EXCUSE #1

"I'm sorry I have to work late."

The Wrong Response • "I'm sorry I have to terminate our friendship early!"

The Right Response • "I understand the non-stop demands of such a high-powered position. Why don't you come for coffee and desert if you finish before 10 P.M.?"

CANCELLATION EXCUSE #2

"I hate doing this but I'm not well."

The Wrong Response • "I've been telling you that for years but it never stopped you from eating my free food before."

The Right Response • "There's a terrible flu bug going around. I had it myself. Don't worry about the party. Just take care of yourself."

CANCELLATION EXCUSE #3

"If I don't have dinner with my mother-in-law my husband will divorce me."

The Wrong Response • "You hate your mother-in-law, your husband is boring, and you live in a community property state. I don't see the problem."

The Right Response • "I respect your sense of duty to your family.

The Saint's Response • "Why don't bring your mother-in-law?"

◆ **Cancellation considerations**

1. Beware of the guest who habitually cancels at the last minute. Some people constantly alter their plans at a moment's notice. Once I am aware of the pattern I only invite these spontaneously spirited individuals to large parties and buffets—*never* to a formal sit-down dinner or luncheon.

2. If you are the type of person who has a habit of canceling at the last minute (for whatever reason) remember that your host or hostess has gone to a great deal of trouble; in all fairness (and for the sake of good manners) you should either (a) not accept the invitation if you have any doubts about attending or (b) make every effort to attend. If you cancel at the last minute it is always a good idea to telephone the next day or send a card apologizing and inquiring about the party. Your thoughtfulness will encourage the host to invite you again in the near future.

◆ How to handle no-shows

HOW LONG TO WAIT

If I entertain a small group for dinner and designate 7:30 P.M. as the arrival time I usually serve between 8:30 and 8:45 P.M. Most of my guests will have arrived by 8 P.M. Allowing 30–45 minutes for a cocktail hour, the food should be on the table no later than 9 P.M. If by 8:45 P.M. one of my guests is missing (and hasn't telephoned) I call the person. In most cases you'll get an answering machine. I leave a message stating the time, my curiosity regarding the absence and my concern for his (or her) well-being. If the cocktail hour is going well, I wait an additional fifteen minutes (in case the potential no-show is about to show-up) and then seat my guests.

*WHAT TO DO WHEN YOU DECIDE
THEY'RE NOT COMING*

Once you've decided that one or more of your guests is a no-show, remove the necessary table setting(s), placecard(s) and chair(s). Do not reset the entire table, however. If, for any reason, the no-show arrives at some later point it would be awkward trying to squeeze the individual into the reset table. As with unexpected guests (see "Unexpected Guests") remain calm and try not to let last-minute changes alter your entertaining style in a negative manner.

WHAT TO DO IF A "NO-SHOW" SHOWS UP!

If two hours into your dinner party, the door bell rings and the no-show arrives, welcome him with open arms. I believe that, no matter what, you should always treat your guests in a hospitable manner. *Always rise above rude behavior.* Make light of your guest's tardy arrival. Congratulate him on arriving in time to watch you flambé the dessert. Although you (and your punctual guests) will be expecting a riveting tale about the late arrival don't ask any questions; allow your guest to offer the information. Quickly reset the place setting with a minimal amount of fuss, emphasizing the fact that you're so glad to see your "lost" friend.

FUTURE INVITATIONS?

Deciding whether to extend future invitations to a no-show is a personal choice. I make my decision on a case-by-case basis, waiting a few days to see if the no-show telephones with an explanation. Unlike Lady Lavistock (who believes that death is the only acceptable excuse), I realize that exceptional circumstances may have prevented the guest from telephoning. But if that individual never offers an explanation or, in any way, acknowledges the absence, I reluctantly remove the name from future guest lists.

No-shows fail to realize that just as a host assumes certain responsibilities when *extending* an invitation, a guest also assumes certain responsibilities by *accepting* the invitation; a commitment to arrive is certainly at the top of that list.

Candles & Incense

Candles and Incense provide two functions when entertaining:

1. *They help to* enhance an atmosphere or mood; *and*

2. *They release a variety of fragrances which* mask cooking odors.

Candles are a simple, elegant, and inexpensive way to transform an ordinary dinner party into something special. Don't underestimate the importance of effectively lighting a room when entertaining. (See "Lighting.") Whether you are using

a set of massive candelabras for a formal dinner party or a collection of small votives placed around the periphery of a room, candles can provide a creative substitute for traditional lighting.

Many people associate incense with either religion (because of its use in certain churches) or sixties pop-culture (flower children, psychedelic drugs and peace signs). They don't realize that this ancient means of perfuming the air can play an important role in everyday entertaining.

◆ Candles

When I organized dinner parties in formal households for such aristocrats as the Marquis and Marchioness of Northampton, I would instruct the staff to polish and set a series of twelve solid gold candelabras across an eighty-foot Hepplewhite dining table. Each candelabra held twelve candles and stood three feet tall. When all 144 tapers were lit each table setting shimmered; the room had a fairy-tale like glow. Unfortunately, because of the size of the candelabras, it was difficult for guests to see each other, let alone speak. Can you imagine trying to make polite conversation across a table while peering through a two-inch gap? Don't use objects—no matter how beautiful—that inhibit a guest's ability to be seen or heard.

I prefer small votive candles to the traditional long tapered variety. Votives are small circular candles which can vary in diameter between one to six inches. They should be placed in glass holders, which prevent them from dripping onto the table surface. These holders vary in style and color and can range in cost from two to two hundred dollars. A collection of three or four small votives placed around a simple floral centerpiece is an elegant and simple way of enhancing any table setting. You'll find that by reducing the overhead lighting and using candles you can create an atmosphere of intimacy that will encourage your guests to relax and enjoy themselves.

◆ Enhancing a mood

Candles are a fun and creative way to make your guests feel as if they are sharing something special. Depending upon the particular occasion (and your imagination) you can create a memorable atmosphere that will set you apart from other hosts. The following suggestions demonstrate how candles can be used for a variety of occasions:

Romantic Dinners • Try a variation on the traditional candle placed in an empty Chianti bottle or glass and brass candlesticks. Find a favorite photograph of a loved one or a seductive image in a magazine. Glue or tape the picture on an empty bottle and place a candle in the opening. For such special occasions as engagement dinners or anniversaries, create a college of copies of treasured photographs that commemorate the events which have led to the party.

Holidays • Halloween and Christmas are perfect holidays for incorporating candles into centerpieces. Use creatively carved pumpkins and evergreens as candleholders for votives.

Summer Entertaining • Pineapples, apples and melons that have been cored down the middle make wonderful candle holders. I once organized a Fourth of July party that featured two halved watermelons carved to resemble battleships; candles were inserted as the mastheads and lettuce leaves were "sails." The cost was minimal and the effect was very entertaining—especially for the children.

I also use incense to enhance a particular mood I may be trying to create—especially during the holidays. During the Christmas season I light incense scented with evergreen or frankincense. When combined with Christmas decorations and carols, incense helps to complete the perfect holiday picture. Remember that when entertaining guests, you are trying to stimulate them on a variety of sensory levels; the sense of smell should not be neglected.

Based upon personal preferences, certain types of incense may be used to perfume the air with a seductive smell for a romantic dinner. Flowered fragrances are often popular but must be used sparingly. If you choose a type of incense that produces a heavily scented aroma, place the incense in a remote part of your home, allowing the scent to subtly waft into the main entertaining areas without overpowering the air.

◆ Masking cooking odors

I often use scented candles to mask certain cooking odors. Although they come in a variety of scents I prefer the fresh spring flower aroma of Cherchez candles. At $25 per candle, however, these are not as economical as the scented varieties available in local candle and card shops. I always light scented candles two hours before my guests are scheduled to arrive, placing them in various rooms to create an overall aroma throughout my home. When entertaining weekend guests, I arrange candles in a variety of locations around the guest bedroom, powder room and bathtub.

I also use incense to mask pungent cooking odors. The aromas produced by certain foods can be overpowering; they can color your event in ways you may not have intended. To avoid this I recommend lighting incense just before you begin cooking.

◆ Outdoor use

For outdoor entertaining, I recommend the use of citronellas. When lit, these candles release an aroma that repels bugs— especially in the evening. Citronellas offer a more civilized approach than "bug zappers" (electronic devices that attract and literally fry insects). I have always found it most unappetizing to attend outdoor dinner parties that are punctuated by the periodic snap, crackle and pop of bugs which have been trapped in the torturous electronic device.

◆ Safety tips

1. Make a list of every candle you light and where you have placed it. At the end of your party or before leaving your home, check the list to ensure that you have not left a candle burning somewhere.

2. If you are entertaining children make sure that the candles are well out of the reach of playful hands.

3. When using glass or crystal votive holders, check them periodically to see how far the candles have burned. If the wax has burned to the bottom and the glass becomes too hot the holder may shatter or ruin the table surface on which it rests.

4. When using candles in the powder room do not place them on top of the commode. I once attended a party where a lady ran screaming out of the bathroom: the hostess was unaware of this most important safety tip; when the unfortunate guest tilted her head backward her hair caught on fire. She gave new meaning to the term "flaming redhead."

5. Using candles with evergreens for Christmas entertaining requires extreme caution. The evergreens should be sprayed periodically with water to keep them as moist and as flame-resistant as possible. They should never be placed in an unattended area.

Candles are like flowers and fine wine: their poetic quality can seduce the reluctant guest, transforming a "wallflower" into a captivating conversationalist.

◆ **The two basic types of incense**

Stick • Stick incense, the most popular and easiest to use, is usually sold in packs containing a dozen pieces. Light the end of the stick and allow it to burn for a few seconds; then blow out the flame and place the stick in an incense burner—usually a long, narrow piece of wood with small holes. If you don't own an incense burner place the burning stick in a potted plant or a Styrofoam cup—but make certain you leave enough room at the bottom so the incense does not burn the cup. Available in a wide variety of fragrances, stick incense can be bought in card stores, health food shops and certain book stores. My favorite type of incense (which I use exclusively in my home) is Blue Willow Champa, which produces the very delicate smell of a spring day.

Charcoal/Resin • This type of incense is frequently found in churches. Although it can be used in the home, care must be taken because it can produce a great deal of smoke. You'll need to purchase the type of charcoal that is specially made for burning resin incense. These small spheres, approximately 1½" in diameter, are sold in most bookstores that specialize in Eastern studies. Place a piece of the charcoal in a cup-like, heat-resistant incense burner and light it with a match. Once the charcoal starts to burn, blow out the flame. Next, place a very small piece of the resin (usually frankincense or myrrh) on top of the charcoal. The key here is to add pieces very gradually because the incense produces a heavy smoke. I once attended a party where someone was using this type of incense for the first time. The hostess, a self-proclaimed "frankincense fanatic," poured the entire contents of a package into the burner. Smoke begin to erupt from the small pot like lava from a volcano. Within seconds the entire room was filled with thick, perfumed clouds. If you decide to use this type of incense I recommend lighting it an hour before your guests arrive, allowing it to burn out before the first person rings the bell. You'll find that the odor will linger in the air for a long time.

If you've never tried incense, experiment with different types and fragrances on your own until you find one you like. Never combine the use of incense with scented candles—it overpowers the air. And be sensitive to individuals who may be allergic to smoke or react negatively to the smell of incense.

Caterers

Anyone who saw the 1992 Steve Martin remake of *Father of the Bride* may have decided that hiring a caterer is a terrifying experience that transforms a happy home into a three-ring circus. Left to their own imaginations (and no budget), caterers occasionally get "catered away." But if you set specific boundaries ("no swans on the front lawn") and define your entertaining needs you will find that these professional party planners can provide invaluable assistance.

◆ Deciding when to hire a caterer

Most caterers accept assignments ranging from an intimate and elegant dinner party for four to a formal sit-down dinner-dance for four hundred. People frequently turn to caterers for assistance when a special occasion for a large group looms on the horizon—weddings, engagements, anniversaries, graduations or retirement parties. These events require tremendous planning and organization. Very few homes have kitchen facilities that can accommodate meal preparation for large groups. A caterer can provide an anxiety-free alternative when you have neither the time nor the inclination to cook. If your budget allows, caterers can be a time-saving option for holiday entertaining when the thought of preparing a Christmas dinner for twenty friends and relatives is over-whelming. Or, if you've invited twelve business associates for cocktails and hors d'oeuvre, why not hire a caterer to agonize over the appetizers so you can dedicate yourself to deal-making. I recommend hiring a caterer if (a) for whatever reason, you aren't capable of executing the party on your own, or (b) the event is of sufficient importance to you (for either personal or professional reasons) that you want to be completely free to socialize.

◆ Questions to answer

Before you begin the process of hiring a caterer ask yourself the following questions. Your answers will assist the caterer in developing a proposal and providing you with an accurate price quote. If you don't know what you want, the caterer will be more than happy to make suggestions but, as was the case in *Father of the Bride*, beware of seductive options that may entice you into exceeding your budget.

WHAT TYPE OF FUNCTION DO I WANT TO HAVE?

Options Include • A sit-down dinner, buffet, cocktail party with hors d'oeuvres, champagne and dessert reception, picnic, clambake, luau—the possibilities are endless. A competent caterer should be able to offer suggestions for each idea.

How Many? • The size of the group should be determined according to space and budget. Never invite more guests than you can comfortably accommodate.

Formal vs. Informal? • Based on the guest list and the purpose of the party, decide whether formal dress will enhance or inhibit the occasion. Black-tie or "fancy" dress can elevate an ordinary cocktail party into a special event but may not be suitable for functions where the majority of people on the guest list do not own formal evening wear.

Indoor/Outdoor? • If you have the space and the season allows, outdoor entertaining is a charming alternative—especially when enlisting the help of a caterer.

WHAT IS MY CATERING BUDGET?

Caterers generally charge per person, with a minimum, for special events like clambakes. Your budget should be based on (a) how many people you're going to invite, (b) what type of event you're going to have, and (c) the quality of food you wish to serve. A very elegant dinner for four can cost the same as a cocktail party for sixteen. Most caterers will give you a list of different suggested menus with a per person price for each. If you want to serve lobster instead of chicken you're obviously going to pay more. Once you've decided on a budget, quote the caterer a figure which is 15–20 percent lower. You will invariably be seduced by irresistible choices that increase the cost of the event. If you begin by quoting a lower figure you have a better chance of not exceeding the budget.

HOW DO I FIND A CATERER?

Personal Experience • If you attend a successful private party or wedding reception, or visit a restaurant that serves remarkable food, find out who's responsible. Keep a list for future events that may require the services of a caterer.

Recommendations from Friends • Don't be shy about asking friends and acquaintances for recommendations. "Word-of-mouth" is how most caterers receive their assignments.

Newspaper and Magazine Articles • Compile a clip-file of articles on catering as they appear in local publications.

Yellow Pages • I use this as a last resort because it provides a minimal amount of detailed information.

◆ **Questions to ask**

Caterers are very accommodating; they will build an entire event around your choices. Be very specific, however, about what you need, what the caterer will deliver, and what it will cost so that there are no surprises or misunderstandings along the way. The following is a list of proposed questions for interviewing caterers:

1. What services does the fee include?

2. What items (china, glass, silver, linens, etc.) are provided?

3. What type of kitchen equipment/space is required; do they have portable kitchens?

4. Decorations?

5. Flowers?

6. Musical arrangements?

7. Is the set-up and clean-up inclusive?

8. What is the deposit/cancellation policy?

9. Hiring extra help?

10. Tipping?

11. References: What type of functions similar to the one you are planning has the prospective caterer organized? Can the caterer provide you with names and telephone numbers so that you can speak to satisfied clients?

12. Ask yourself if the prospective caterer inspires trust.

Remember that you're hiring a caterer to perform a particular service that you do not want to perform. Once all of the specifics have been agreed upon, allow the caterer to do his (or her) job; don't interfere with or second guess every decision. If you are the type of person who is uncomfortable delegating responsibility or entrusting the overall success of a party to a stranger, don't hire a caterer. Enlist the help of friends or relatives (or hired help) who will work under your direct supervision. A strained relationship between a host and the caterer will ultimately affect the overall party atmosphere.

Caviar

Many people regard caviar as the food of the gods; with prices reaching up to $400 a pound you might well think you have to be connected to people in high places to be able to afford a few precious ounces. Budgetary considerations aside, caviar inspires extreme love/hate relationships. For some guests, the thought of socializing in the presence of "fish eggs" is revolting; for others, nothing could be more exhilarating than the initial glimpse of "black gold": that tongue-tingling moment of euphoric anticipation, fantasizing about the first sinfully indulgent spoonful.

◆ What is caviar?

Caviar is the processed roe of female sturgeons caught in the Black and Caspian seas. While there are a variety of popular and less expensive products produced from the roe of salmon (frequently used in the preparation of sushi), lumpfish, whitefish, and carp, these products are not considered true caviar. The United States and France have laws restricting what can be termed "caviar." In France only the processed roe of sturgeon

> "Caviar is more than a food, it's a dream."
> —Christian Petrossian

may be called caviar. In the United States, however, a product can be called "caviar" as long as the label clearly states the type of fish from which the eggs originated. *When purchasing caviar always ask questions and read labels to determine exactly what you're getting.*

◆ The 3 types of caviar considered to be "the best"

Although the debate over "the best caviar" is never-ending the following types are generally considered to be worth the investment. The prices quoted are from Zabar's—a popular New York food shop that always offers quality caviar at competitive prices. If you are going to buy caviar, shop around—the cost can vary dramatically.

Beluga • (Average price: 7 oz. jar—$135; 4 oz. jar—$75) This sizable fish can grow to be 12 feet in length and weigh 800 pounds. Its eggs (3 millimeters in diameter) are the largest and have a very subtle flavor. The color ranges from light to dark gray, based on the time of year the fish is caught: the eggs become lighter in color the nearer the spawning time.

Osetra • (Average price: 7 oz. jar—$70; 4 oz. jar—$40) Almost half the size of beluga, the osetra grows to approximately six feet and can weigh up to 400 pounds. The eggs are brownish gray with a yellow or gold tint and are characterized by a slightly fruity flavor.

Sevruga • (Average price: 7 oz. jar—$60; 4 oz. jar—$35) The sevruga grows to be a few feet in length and averages 50 pounds. Its eggs are dark gray to black and have a strong flavor.

◆ **Buying and storing**

Estimating one ounce of caviar per person, purchase as much as you think you'll need for a single event. While an unopened tin or jar of caviar will keep for a month, anything left over will perish in a few days. Fresh caviar is characterized by a shiny, almost sparkling quality and a clarity of color—if it looks cloudy it's not fresh. The eggs should be distinctly separated—not pressed together or burst. Caviar spoils quickly. No matter how short the ride home make sure the container is packed in an insulated bag. When properly packaged, caviar can travel for up to twelve hours. I have had caviar shipped to me in various locations via Federal Express without any problems. Be sure to open the overnight package as soon as it arrives and immediately store the unopened caviar in the refrigerator.

◆ **Serving caviar**

Caviar Dish • If you enjoy caviar and plan on serving it more than once every five years, invest in a proper caviar dish. Made of glass or fine crystal, a caviar dish is similar in concept to a double boiler: a small dish (containing the caviar) rests inside a larger dish filled with ice. When served in a proper dish, caviar is quite safe for several hours.

"Makeshift" Caviar Dish • If you are experimenting with caviar for the first time and do not want to invest in a proper caviar dish, create your own. Find two matching glass bowls of unequal sizes or use a shot glass with a beautiful china soup bowl underneath. Be creative.

Caviar Spoon • I prefer using a mother-of-pearl spoon which is not only beautiful but doesn't tarnish or corrode like silver from the salt content of the caviar. Whatever you choose, it should be elegant. An actress I know once told me, "Nothing gets between me and my caviar." She then tossed a large spoonful into the palm of her hand and scooped it out with her tongue!

On the Side • Caviar is traditionally served on toast points (toasted bread cut into triangles with the crusts removed). When serving caviar as an appetizer or for a first course you may substitute blinis (small pancakes) for the toast points. Americans are fond of serving chopped egg, onion and sour cream on the side but I find these toppings mask the taste—and finely chopped onion is not the most desirable aroma when entertaining.

Accompanying Beverages • Iced vodka or champagne are the two beverages of choice when serving caviar. Other types of liquor either mask or obscure the subtle flavors.

◆ Caviar considerations

1. An opened jar or tin of caviar will only keep in the refrigerator for a few days. If you have left-over caviar store it in the front part of your refrigerator where you won't forget about it. Once when my mother was visiting from England I had a small cocktail party and served champagne and caviar to celebrate her arrival. At the end of the party she insisted on helping me clean. I never saw her place the left-over Beluga in a china tea cup covered with foil on the side shelf of my refrigerator. Imagine my horror a week later when I found the container and discovered $200 worth of spoiled fish eggs.

2. If you are interested in trying caviar but are intimidated by the price, experiment with the less expensive types (salmon, whitefish, lumpfish)—many of which are produced in the United States.

3. If you cook with caviar or combine it with other foods don't use the most expensive types. Remember that processed caviar contains salt, and adjust your recipes accordingly.

4. Some of your guests might be intimidated by serving themselves; most people who have never had caviar would rather go without than risk embarrassing themselves. To make my guests comfortable, I always ask, "May I serve you some?"

Centerpieces

Nothing is more complimentary to a well-set table than a magnificent centerpiece. Just as a pair of diamond earrings can enhance a beautiful face, a carefully executed centerpiece synthesizes an assortment of silver, china and crystal into a stunning image. Conversely, a centerpiece that is not harmonious with the table setting can destroy hours of hard work. Many years ago I catered a society wedding for Lady Lavistock—a family friend. The celebration was held in the garden of her country estate in a tiny hamlet in the Cotswolds. Lady Lavistock was an extremely opinionated woman; although we agreed upon an arrangement of round banquet tables draped in peach silk, our centerpiece ideas were quite different. I envisioned a low arrangement of white and peach roses; she had an "inspiration" of three-foot topiaries sculpted into the shape of a bride and bridegroom. I tried to point out that socializing through shrubs—no matter how skillfully sculpted—could prove challenging but Lady Lavistock was undeterred.

A team of gardeners worked for days to create (what must still be) one of the most unusual collections of centerpieces ever presented at a wedding. Despite the unorthodox arrangements the reception proceeded smoothly. Halfway through the dessert course, however, the sky began to fill with clouds; in a matter of seconds the weather changed. Gusts as swift and sharp as karate chops swept through the garden, toppling the collection of "happy couples." Lady Lavistock began to scream while the guests ran for cover. A few minutes later the sky cleared; the winds died down. With the help of several amused butlers I removed the sizable centerpieces; the reception continued.

The following rules can help a centerpiece bring your guests together—not (as in the case with Lady Lavistock)—send them running for cover.

◆ 5 rules for successful centerpieces

Centerpieces Should Not Be Too Tall • Although massive centerpieces can be very dramatic on a buffet table they should be lower than eye-level on a dining table. Dinner parties are about socializing—not staring at or peeking through a wall of flowers. Anything that inhibits conversation should be eliminated.

Centerpieces Should Not Be Too Wide • I have been seated at numerous dining tables that feature flowers, leaves, and other assorted items spilling into my dinner plate or water glass. Trying to find a fork in the foliage is like hunting for truffles? Allow at least two inches between the centerpiece and the table setting so that a guest can lift a glass or a fork without knocking something over.

Centerpieces Should Not Compete with or Overpower a Table Setting • In size and design, a centerpiece should not detract from the beauty of a well-set table. Try to achieve a harmonious relationship between all of the items so that no single item stands out. A well-executed centerpiece is like a piece of fine jewelry that adorns but does not overpower its wearer.

Centerpieces Should Not Be Vulgar • Vulgar centerpieces are characterized by: ostentatious or oversized arrangements (Lady Lavistock's topiary centerpieces); the use of brash or incongruous colors; props that are inappropriate for the occasion. Several years ago a New York society matron organized a dinner honoring America's finest writers. She had an inspiration to incorporate the individual author's books into the centerpieces. As if trivializing the writer's work into a decorative prop wasn't bad enough, she also had the book jackets lightly spray-painted in gold to match the overall decor. Many of the guests who attended the dinner were offended by such a lack of respect for both authors and books.

Centerpieces Should Enhance the Mood, Theme or Occasion • Whether you're organizing a romantic dinner for two, a children's birthday party, or a New Year's Day brunch, the centerpiece should capture the spirit of the occasion. Choose specific colors to coincide with seasons or holidays. If possible, incorporate the favorite flower of your special guest into the centerpiece.

Centerpieces Should Be Safe • Because your guests are close to a centerpiece, make sure they can in no way harm themselves. Arrangements that combine candles with foliage or use objects or flowers with sharp edges and thorns need to be carefully examined. Outdoor centerpieces require special attention because of the uncontrollable elements—weather, wind and bugs.

◆ Centerpiece suggestions

EASTER

- Create a simple arrangement of daffodils.

- Fill a basket with painted eggs and cut hyacinths in oases (an absorbent foam used by florists).

- Paint a wooden box and plant it with tulips.

- Make a large egg-shaped centerpiece by paper machéing a balloon; pop the balloon after the paper dries and cut the egg shape in half; fill each half with greenery, dried flowers or dyed eggs.

VALENTINE'S DAY

- Buy or make small red paper hearts and glue them onto a basket filled with heart-shaped candies or red baby roses.

- Cut a heart-shaped centerpiece out of Styrofoam and decorate it with dried flowers, ribbons, and a picture of your loved one.

HALLOWEEN

- Carve pumpkins (either traditional faces or abstract patterns) and then paint them in a variety of *vibrant colors; place a small votive candle inside to highlight your design.*

THANKSGIVING

● *Use a mixture of pine cones, fruit, cabbages, and nuts to make a colorful centerpiece either in a basket or spread down the table center.*

CHRISTMAS

● *Decorate a log with pine cones, holly and berries.*

● *Fill a small basket with dried flowers and pine cones.*

● *Wrap a beautiful present and drape it with beads and pearls; incorporate white tulips or roses into the design.*

● *Create your own miniature Christmas trees out of Styrofoam cones; decorate the shapes with whatever inspires you (old costume jewelry, loose beads or rhinestones. . . .*

No matter what you choose, being creative and enjoying the process is the key to successful centerpieces. Page through magazines; take mental notes or tear out pictures of arrangements you find appealing. Visit flower shops for ideas to adapt. You can have tremendous fun including family members. If you have children, make the creation of the Thanksgiving or Christmas centerpiece a family project.

Champagne

Champagne is my favorite drink—and one that's often misunderstood. Most people regard champagne as a luxury item—something to be sipped once a year on New Year's Eve. You may not realize that serving champagne for any occasion can simplify your work load while enhancing a particular mood. I serve champagne exclusively whenever I entertain—brunch, lunch, dinner, cocktails, for a "nightcap" or anything in between.

◆ 6 reasons why champagne is suitable for any occasion

1. It allows you to spend more time with your guests. Instead of juggling a variety of liquors, sodas, juices, glasses, garnishes and ice to make individuals drinks, all you have to do is open a bottle and pour.

2. It makes people feel special—as if they've been invited into an episode of "Lifestyles of the Rich and Famous." The next time you're entertaining friends "pop open a bottle of bubbly" and watch their faces light up.

3. You can save money by purchasing good, inexpensive champagne instead of stocking a bar with liquor, sodas and juices.

4. It's easier to monitor the alcohol level of your guests: Keep track of how many bottles you've served and in what amount of time.

5. It unites your guests. Champagne is a stimulus for toast-making. One of the most effective methods for bringing a group together is to make a toast, expressing a specific sentiment for a particular occasion.

6. It's wonderfully seductive. The next time you want to make an amorous impression, open a bottle of champagne. If your acquaintance asks "What's the special occasion?," answer with something complimentary like "being in the presence of someone so special."

Champagne is an acidic sparkling wine produced in a northern region of France appropriately called "Champagne." In France, unlike in America, only sparkling wines that come from this particular region may be called champagne. The difference between champagne and sparkling wine is the production process. French champagne is created through a complex and time-consuming method called Méthode Champenoise. Sparkling wines are processed more simply. The fermentation process often takes place in large vats (instead of in the bottle) and chemicals like sulfates may be used to speed the process. *Always read labels carefully to find out how the champagne was processed and if it contains chemicals.*

People who do not serve champagne on a regular basis are often intimidated when they want to make a purchase. They are either worried about the expense or unfamiliar with the various types.

The first three considerations when purchasing champagne are size, quantity and quality. For most occasions, standard bottles are preferable. But you should be aware that champagne is sold in a variety of bottle sizes. I usually estimate 2–3 glasses per person when deciding how many bottles to purchase. Some guests will consume more, some less; it all evens out.

Sizes of Champagne Bottles

Split:	2 glasses	Rehoboam:	6 bottles
Half-bottle:	3 glasses	Methuselah:	8 bottles
Bottle:	6 glasses	Salmanzar:	12 bottles
Magnum:	2 bottles	Balthazar:	16 bottles
Jeroboam:	4 bottles	Nebuchadnezzar:	20 bottles

Magnums are fun for very special occasions but require dexterity when pouring. I once catered a wedding for an eccentric Englishwoman who insisted we use Nebuchadnezzars. The poor waiters! It required four men to lift the monstrosities. And the first few glasses usually ended up on the floor or in someone's lap.

The type of champagne you purchase will be influenced by your budget, taste preference (dry, extra dry, sweet) and how you will be serving the champagne. If you're mixing it with orange juice to make mimosas, choose an inexpensive champagne. The following is a recommendation of champagnes listed from inexpensive to expensive. You'll find better bargains at large discount outlets than your neighborhood store, so shop around and compare prices.

Brand Names	Average Cost
Freixenet	$3.99
Codorniu	5.99
Paul Cheneau (Blanc de Blancs)	6.49
Segura Viudas Brut NV	6.99
Segura Aria Brut	9.99
Korbel	9.99
Chandon (Blanc de Noirs)	9.99
Moët & Chandon (White Star)	19.99
Perrier-Jouët	19.99
G.H. Mumm & Co.	21.99
Moët & Chandon (Brut)	23.99
Taittinger	24.99
Veuve Cliquot	27.99
Dom Perignon	78.99
Louis Roederer Cristal	99.99

◆ How to chill champagne

Champagne should be chilled in the refrigerator for at least three hours. Fifteen minutes before your guests arrive, place the bottle in a champagne bucket. If you're going to serve champagne more than once a year you should invest in a bucket. Inexpensive glass and metal shapes ($20–$40) are sold at most houseware stores. Elaborate silver and gold plated styles are available for thousands of dollars at exclusive shops like Tiffany's or Christofle.

Fill three-quarters of the champagne bucket with ice cubes. (You can add a bit of water at the bottom to speed the chilling process.) The bottle should be submerged halfway in the bucket—not sitting atop a mountain of ice. If you're pressed for time you can place the bottle in the freezer for ten minutes. The great danger obviously lies in forgetting to take it out. I once attended a birthday party where a guest brought a vintage bottle of Dom and insisted it be opened even though the champagne was not properly chilled. The hostess cleverly placed the gift in the freezer and set the stove-top timer for ten minutes. Unfortunately, amid the clatter of the party she never heard the bell. Thirty minutes later everyone within a three-block radius must have been startled by what sounded like a gun shot. The bottle exploded in the freezer, creating a horrible mess and a terrible waste. So remember, if you have to put a bottle in the freezer tell at least five people to remind you or you might find yourself in a similar dilemma.

◆ **Important considerations when serving champagne**

Glasses • Champagne should be served in either flute (v-shaped) or tulip (u-shaped) glasses. Many years ago, very wide, saucer shaped glasses were popular. A tall, thin glass, however, is preferable for retaining the champagne's bubbly quality. There are a variety of quality plastic glasses on the market that are affordable and practical for outdoor entertaining. For informal occasions I use inexpensive glass flutes ($14.95 for a set of four). When entertaining more formally I prefer the Cartier tulip glasses ($125 each). I recently saw a magnificent pair of Erté champagne glasses but at $500 a pair you'd have to have a very carefree attitude about breakages.

Uncorking the Bottle • Contrary to what we see on television a bottle of champagne should not explode upon opening with foam sputtering and splashing everyone in sight. Hold the bottle securely with one hand and gradually twist the cork in a clock-wise direction with the other hand. The most important thing to remember when opening a bottle of champagne is to make certain the cork is pointed away from you, your guests and anything of value in your home. I attended a dinner party in New York where a gregarious host became distracted while opening a magnum of Moët; he neglected to keep his hand over the cork. Imagine his surprise when the cork shot out of the bottle and landed in the middle of a treasured Picasso.

Pouring • Fill a glass two-thirds full to allow the foam to rise; then top it off until the glass is three-quarters full. Wrap the bottom of the bottle with a white linen napkin to absorb moisture and provide you with a better grip when pouring. As with wine, the bottle label should be facing toward the guest so he can see the brand of champagne being served. Always remember to return the bottle to the bucket after pouring to keep it chilled.

Everyone has a favorite drink. For some it may be a good brandy; for others, a fine wine. I have always been an enthusiast of the exotic elixir with the sparkling bubbles: champagne. Not just a drink but a way of life.

Cleaning Up

Picture it: you wave fondly good-bye to your last dinner guest; you are slightly tipsy, tired, and ready for bed. The moment after the front door closes, terror strikes! You suddenly realize that your once perfectly spotless home has been transformed into an official EDA ("Entertainment Disaster Area"); every kitchen surface is covered with pots, pans, dishes, plates, glasses, knives, forks, spoons, and a sampling of the evening's menu. The living and dining rooms look as if a hurricane just swept through. After realizing that you don't qualify for federal assistance, you begin to hyperventilate as you look at (a) your spouse, (b) your loved one, (c) your pet, or, (d) your horrified reflection in the mirror, trying to remember who talked you into the idiotic idea of entertaining friends!

For many people, the thought of having to clean up after a dinner party is a nightmare. It is possible, however, with some thought and organization, to shorten the cleaning process. During my many years of service organizing hundreds of parties, I have devised a method for expediting this most unpleasant task. If you incorporate the following suggestions I guarantee that you will be able to tidy up after any function in thirty minutes or less.

◆ Desmond's amazing 30-minute clean-up

The most important rule of cleaning up is to do as much of the cleaning as possible before your guests arrive. If you don't start with an immaculate kitchen, bathroom, living or dining room, you only increase the amount of work you have to do at the end of the evening. Before the evening begins make sure to do the following:

- *Wash, dry and return to storage all cooking utensils (pots, pans, etc.) that have been used in preparation of the meal.*

- *Clean the sink, stove and all of the counter tops where you have been working.*

- *Empty the dishwasher to ensure maximum stacking capacity.*

- *Empty all garbage containers.*

Unless you have help, choose a menu that does not require complicated, last-minute cooking. This will reduce the amount of pots and pans that have to be washed at the end of the evening. (See "Menu Planning.")

While your guests are being seated at the dinner table, quickly tidy the living room of empty glasses, hors d'oeuvres, plates, and napkins. Plates should be stacked in the dishwasher; paper napkins should be tossed in the garbage bin, cloth or linen should be arranged in a pile for later laundering. Fluff up the pillows and straighten the furniture. If possible, ask your spouse or a very close friend to assist you. I believe it's helpful to clear this area so that after dinner, should your guests choose to have coffee and tea in the living room, they don't have to face an area strewn with dirty glasses and plates.

During dinner, use the approach outlined in "Serving and Clearing the Table" to ensure that you don't face a kitchen strewn with plates at the end of the evening. The key to shortening the tidying up process is to clean as you go, working your way through the event.

Spot-check bathrooms throughout the evening. One evening, I entertained of group of high-profile people in the entertainment industry. Just before we sat down to dinner I noticed one of my guests (a well-known actress in a now canceled television series) emerge from the bathroom with an entirely different hair style. My curiosity was aroused: I examined the bathroom and found water, hair and towels everywhere! She must have looked in the mirror, had an inspiration and decided she couldn't wait to re-style herself.

After your guests have left, the only remaining items to be washed should be a few pots, the silver and some glasses. Empty the garbage so that the odor of leftover food does not linger throughout your home.

Use a methodical approach, rather than a random, haphazard way of wandering around the room. Two popular methods include: "the clock approach" wherein you designate a particular spot (dining table) as twelve o'clock and then methodically work your way clockwise through the entertaining space; or "the room-by-room" approach wherein you clean one room at a time, section by section. If you have help, delegate responsibilities, assigning the other person a particular room so that you don't get in each other's way.

Since the experts have yet to invent a silent vacuum cleaner, I usually leave this task until the next day. If the hour is late, my neighbors are asleep, and my head is still echoing the sounds of the evening's conversation, there is more to be lost than gained by plugging in the Electrolux for a round of "dirty dancing."

I never retire for the evening until everything is washed, dried, stored and my home is returned to its original order. I prefer to rise to a clean home than to face even one lipstick-stained glass in the morning.

◆ **Dishwashing**

Deciding when to wash the dishes can be one of the more exasperating decisions for a host. Trying to ensure that (a) your guests are continually entertained, (b) the kitchen does not become cluttered, and (c) your home does not smell like broiled tuna while you are serving apple pie can be a bit of a juggle. But you don't have to hire a magician—just make a plan of attack.

I use a system (see "Serving & Clearing the Table") of rinsing and stacking the dishes (in either the sink or the dishwasher) as soon as they are cleared from the table. This method minimizes your time in the kitchen, maximizes your ability to entertain your guests, helps to reduce lingering food odors, and simplifies the final cleaning process.

Although the process of dishwashing itself requires little explanation, the following may help simplify and organize your approach to this mundane mission the next time you entertain:

- *Always start with an empty* dishwaser. If you begin with a cluttered dishwasher and *then* try and stack dishes during your party you will be forced to either (a) run the dishwaser during the party and then empty its contents to make room, or (b) stack the dishes on the kitchen counter top. Make sure you have dishwashing detergent, soap and towels.

• *Always start with a clean and empty* sink. This will give you room to maneuver when you cook and clean.

• *Before the guests arrive prepare a tub of hot, soapy water to soak silver or other items that should not be placed in a dishwasher.*

• *When stacking dishes (either in the dishwasher or sink) group the plates and glasses by size to maximize the use of the space. Random or haphazard stacking can lead to breakages.*

• *Unless absolutely necessary I do not recommend running a dishwasher until all of the guests* have departed. Most dishwashers produce an assortment of distracting noises.

• *In most instances, if a guest offers to help with the dishes, I politely decline. No matter how well-intended the individual may be, the last place I want a guest to end up is in the kitchen with a towel. Exceptions to this rule include holidays and large family gatherings where dishwashing may be a tradition or means of socializing.*

• *If you are using prized family heirlooms that will require hand washing at the end of the evening, designate a safe place in your kitchen where the precious possessions can be stored when you clear the table.*

● *Always start with a clean towel when drying dishes or glasses by hand. A soiled dish towel can be unhygienic.*

If you find it difficult to implement any of the above suggestions in a *speedy* manner, try another method. Choices that compel you to spend more time in the kitchen and less time with your guests will, ultimately, impede the success of the party.

Coats

A few years ago, I attended a Christmas party in a large Manhattan loft overlooking the Hudson River. When the host—a charming but scattered editor in a major publishing house—offered to take my coat I reluctantly handed him my new black cashmere overcoat. He took a few steps toward a piece of furniture buried under a mountain of winter wear and, with a loud exclamation, tossed my coat onto the pile as if it were a sacrificial offering to the gods of good taste. Although his sloppy approach to "coat check" made me inquisitive about his overall entertaining style I decided to hope for the best.

Several hours later I thanked the host for his hospitality. When he escorted me back to the "coat check" I was horrified. The gods had not been pacified with my sacrificial lamb: the volcano had erupted, spewing an assortment of outerwear in every direction. After several minutes of digging through the debris I finally located my abused cashmere. The silk lining was ripped; there were footprints on the back. The host apologized by remarking, "It must have been a better party than I thought!"—as if the results of this unnatural disaster were evidence of social success.

The following suggestions will alleviate your guests' outerwear anxiety and prevent any "unnatural disasters" from occurring in your home.

◆ Before the guests arrive

Decide Where the Guests' Coats Will Be Placed • Don't wait until a group is standing in the hallway before you realize that your front closet is overflowing with old wrapping paper, a collection of broken umbrellas and a pile of clothes to be sent to the dry cleaner. Plan ahead: designate a coat check location in your home that is easily accessible and doesn't require hours of cleaning.

Make Sure There Is Enough Room in the Designated Closet • Don't overcrowd closets. It's embarrassing to retrieve a guest's coat from a tightly packed space and find two shirts and an umbrella attached.

Make Sure You Have Enough Hangers • This may seem obvious but you'd be surprised at the number of times I've stood in a hallway watching the host flip through every item of clothing in the closet in the hopes of finding a lone hanger hiding in the crowd. The initial moments when a guest arrives set the tone for the occasion. As a guest, I am comforted by the sight of spacious closets and ample hangers.

◆ When the guests arrive

Take Control of the Situation • Many people (especially first-time guests) will specifically wait until the host asks, "May I take your coat?" After you've greeted the guests and exchanged a few pleasantries, offer to assist them with the removal of their coats.

**Develop a Method for Remembering What
Your Guests Wear** • Like a waiter who remembers
"who ordered what" a host who can remember "who wore
what" inspires confidence. With smaller groups this is usually
not a problem. Make a note or compliment the guest on the
coat upon arrival to help you remember.

◆ Coat considerations

If you're having a large party use a guest room closet or an
empty part of your bedroom closet that can easily accommodate all of the coats. Write the guest's name on Post-its
attached to each hanger. Arrange the coats alphabetically
to facilitate their retrieval. If the party is extremely large hire
someone, or perhaps ask a young relative to organize the
coat check. If you don't have sufficient closet space, rent or
buy collapsable coat racks on wheels.

Try not to pile coats on a bed or a sofa. Not only does
it create an ever increasing mess but retrieving the coats can
be a nightmare. And certain fabrics wrinkle when buried
under three feet of winter wear.

To maintain tidy rooms and to prevent items from being
lost or misplaced, discourage guests from tossing their coats
on nearby chairs. Tell them you would hate to see such a
beautiful garment wrinkled; insist on placing it on a hanger.

If one of your guests wears a blazer, jacket or sweater
and removes it later in the evening, offer to hang it up. Your
thoughtful gesture will keep the garment from getting wrinkled and maintain the order of the entertaining space.

If you do not store coats in the front hallway closet but
in another room of your home, let the guests know where you

are placing their coats. It can be very frustrating when you're ready to leave a large party, can't find the host and have absolutely no idea where your coat is.

The most important thing to remember about coats is to *formulate a plan* that will inspire your guests' confidence in your abilities, allowing them to relax and enjoy themselves.

Coffee & Tea

When I lived in England, I attended many formal dinner parties. It was customary at the conclusion of the meal for the ladies to retire to the drawing room, leaving the gentlemen to drink brandy, smoke cigars and tell off-color stories. At the appropriate time the hostess would rise and say, "Ladies, shall we retire to the drawing room?"; the gentlemen would stand until their feminine counterparts had departed. In the drawing room the ladies would have liqueurs (usually sherry) and converse among themselves. After approximately thirty minutes, the gentlemen would rejoin the ladies for coffee, tea and casual conversation.

Although the post-meal coffee and tea ritual of separating the men and women until it was time for coffee and tea is no longer performed with the same pomp and circumstance, it is still observed by many hosts and hostesses in formal households. Although I do not advocate such formality coffee and tea should be served after— not during—the dessert course. Many hosts make the transition by specifically asking, "Would anyone like coffee or tea?" The unprepared host secretly hopes that the group will respond with a resounding "No": after muddling through a three-course dinner; he or she may find it difficult to muster the enthusiasm necessary for cleaning the coffee machine, finding filters, brewing tea, retrieving the cups and saucers, and transporting everything into the living room. The prepared host, however, is fearless—even when the response includes: "two black coffees—one decaffeinated; one with milk and sugar (and caffeine); one with milk and Sweet-n-Low (and caffeine); and two teas."

I always prepare both coffee and tea an hour before my dinner guests arrive, then keep them warm in attractive thermoses that are not only decorative but functional. Thermoses can retain heat for up to six hours, which is plenty of time unless you have marathon dinner parties. Although the thermoses are available in a variety of styles and colors, I prefer simple shapes that are either silverplated or made of stainless steel.

After you have made your coffee, reset the coffee maker, filling it with water, a filter and coffee grounds so it's ready to go if you need to make more. Coffee purists who require that their coffee be made moments before it is served can still organize everything and wait until the last minute to brew the coffee.

◆ **Prepare a coffee and tea trolley**

After I have brewed the coffee (both decaf and regular) and tea, I organize the cups, saucers, milk, cream, sugar, Sweet-n-Low, liqueurs, and liqueur glasses by placing everything on a movable trolley. If my guests prefer to remain at the dining table I slide the trolley next to the table and serve from there; if they choose to withdraw to another room, I move the trolley to the appropriate location. Movable trolleys are very handy when entertaining and allow for maximum flexibility. Some hosts use them for serving and clearing the table to reduce the amount of trips between the kitchen and the dining room.

◆ Types of coffee

Many supermarket coffees are created by blending a variety of beans from different countries. You can usually find pure coffees (unmixed or unblended) in specialty or gourmet food shops. I rarely purchase coffee beans and grind my own. Because I brew the coffee before my guests arrive the benefit of fresh-ground coffee would be lost. Coffee is best ground just before it is used because the grinding process breaks open the cells of the bean, releasing the aromatic oils. With all of the other entertaining duties to occupy my time, I have learned to persevere with pre-ground. If you are a coffee purist, however, wait until just before you plan on serving the coffee to grind the beans. Always store pre-ground coffee in the freezer to retain its freshness.

INSTANT/FREEZE DRIED

I do not recommend the use of freeze-dried instant coffees for entertaining purposes. Although the flavor of certain brands is quite good, the aromas they produce pale in comparison to freshly made coffee. Part of the after-dinner coffee drinking experience is becoming intoxicated by the aroma.

FLAVORED COFFEES

Pre-ground coffee is available in a variety of flavors such as amaretto, almond, chocolate mint, Irish Whiskey, and orange. If you want to serve something different, try experimenting with mixing your own coffee (combining two different blends) or adding such flavorful spices and liqueurs as cinnamon, nutmeg, cloves, vanilla, ginger, Kahlua (Mexican coffee) or brandy.

The following is a list of popular coffees and the average price per pound:

Type	Price
House Blend	$6
Colombian Supreme	$7
French Roast	$9
Flavored Coffees	$8–$10
Hawaiian Kona	$12
Jamaican High Mountain	$15
Jamaican Blue Mountain	$20
(considered to be the "best" coffee)	

◆ Types of tea

Teas are available in either loose form (which has to be brewed in a pot) or by the bag. The most popular types of tea in America are Earl Grey, Orange Pekoe, Darjeeling and Lapsang souchong. In this increasingly health-conscious age I prepare herbal teas such as chamomile, red zinger and kuchia bancha (a Japanese twig tea). There are dozens of varieties available at your local health food or specialty stores. Loose tea (and tea bags) should be stored in an airtight, lightproof container, at room temperature. Exposure to sunlight or cold storage will rob the tea of its flavor.

◆ Serve it while it's hot

No matter when you decide to prepare the coffee and tea always check the temperature of the liquid before pouring. Coffee and tea should be served hot—not warm. There is no sense in following up a lovely meal with a lukewarm cup of tea or coffee.

Comfort Factor

The rocky road to convivial catastrophes is paved with awkward and impersonal choices. Photographs and suggestions offered in entertainment books should be used to help you discover your own style—not as a blueprint for duplicating such details as the color and placement of the baby's breath in the centerpiece. Inexperienced hosts frequently try to imitate what they see and read instead of picking and choosing what works best for them. Two summers ago I attended a Sunday brunch in Greenwich, Connecticut. The hostess was a charming but socially inexperienced young woman who desperately wanted to make an impression on her guests. She duplicated a chapter from a beautifully photographed book on summer entertaining. Having studied the book, I was amazed at her Xeroxing abilities: she had copied everything from the menu, placemats, china, and glasses to the fruit arrangement in the center of the buffet table. While the display was breathtaking, the hostess was visibly anxious and exhausted by the enormity of her undertaking; although she had created a magnificent picture she didn't have a clue about how to interact with the guests or what to do once the party began. I thought that she was intimidated and overwhelmed by her own presentation. And as the guests began to mar her "perfect

> **"Making comfortable choices is the key to successful entertaining."**
>
> —Countess Eleanor Dudley-Smith

picture" (by eating from the buffet table) she became quite unnerved. Truly successful social events occur when a host feels comfortable enough to share his or her own unique vision of entertaining.

◆ Defining comfort

As with fun (see "Fun Factor"), the definition of comfort varies based upon individual experience and preference. While I am completely relaxed organizing and executing a formal sit-down dinner for twenty-five, most of my friends would require a small staff, a large oxygen tank and a prescription for Valium. Comfortable choices are effortless, worry-free extensions of who you are, how you live, and the style in which you wish to present yourself. While "beer 'n' pizza" parties can be a casual and relaxing way to socialize, I wouldn't be comfortable hosting such an event because it would be incongruous with my personal style. As a general rule, if a choice does not excite you (even if you execute it to complete perfection) it won't relax you. And a nervous host is not conducive to successful socialization.

◆ Making comfortable choices

If you have had little experience entertaining and are uncomfortable with the very idea of being responsible for the nutritional and social well-being of a group of friends, ask yourself the following questions as you begin to develop a plan of attack:

1. Is this something I would look forward to?

2. Does the idea excite me?

3. Do I find the suggestion overwhelming?

4. Can I picture myself engaged in the particular activity?

5. Is this something I would enjoy learning?

6. Would the choice be appropriate for the occasion?

7. Would my guests enjoy the choice?

8. Can I afford to do this?

9. Do I have the time to do this?

These questions can help you make decisions about the size of event, style, menu, and music. For example, if you find the idea of a sit-down dinner intimidating or too formal, organize an elegant buffet. Or, if you have an idea for making a centerpiece but don't have the time, buy some fresh flowers and save your idea for another occasion. Many first-time hosts make the mistake of taking on too much too soon; they end up traumatizing themselves, and reinforcing what may already be a negative attitude about entertaining. If you haven't had a lot of party-planning experience, give yourself a chance by observing the following three suggestions:

1. Start simple.

2. Be realistic about what you can handle.

3. Allow yourself to make mistakes.

◆ Overcoming fears

The best way to overcome a fear of entertaining is to make very specific choices; organize, plan, prepare, and rehearse until you know the routine in your sleep. Surround yourself as much as possible with friends with whom you are comfortable. If you have to entertain anxiety-producing people—new acquaintances, relatives or business associates—include a close friend who has a calming effect (and an extra pair of hands).

◆ Careful experimentation

As you become increasingly comfortable with entertaining begin to expand your horizons in *small* ways. Invite a few friends to a formal three-course dinner party. Have fun with the idea by telling them that you're conducting an experiment; they have the honor of being your "test subjects." Careful experimentation will keep your entertaining style alive, preventing you from becoming bored with the routine.

A successful host is the one who accepts the responsibility of his mission—to seek out new forms of entertainment; to boldly go where no host has gone before—but proceeds with care and caution as he propels himself into the social stratosphere.

Conversation

Lively conversation is at the heart of all successful entertaining; it is an indication that your guests feel comfortable and have relaxed to the point where they can speak freely. No matter how spectacular the table setting, centerpiece, flowers or food, if the group doesn't reach the point of free-flowing conversation the party will feel dead, and your efforts will have been for naught. Party conversation does not have to be an endless string of clever Noel Coward one-liners but it should be characterized by an exchange of up-beat, energetic and enthusiastic ideas. Certain people will sometimes try to manipulate the conversation into directions that you (and your guests) may not find appropriate for the occasion. Such maneuvering may include: an incision-by-incision narrative recounting the painful experience of a recent appendectomy; the salacious details of a spouse's infidelity; diseases; holocausts; wars. Unless you feel certain that your gathering would find these discussions mesmerizing, change the subject.

> **"A highly skilled hostess is like an air traffic controller: she monitors all the pieces of information in the air at any given moment and makes split-second decisions about which news item may land safely at her table."**
>
> **—Desmond Atholl**

◆ Conversational considerations

Making Introductions • As host, your principal social duty is to introduce your guests to one another. Although I am naturally extroverted and have no problem approaching strangers at a party, not everyone is as gregarious. Certain guests may need a "jump start" to rotate their conversational wheels. When entertaining small groups (eight or less) I make formal introductions as the guests arrive; with larger gatherings I offer a few initial introductions and then leave them on their own for awhile. Whenever possible, I try to include a personal detail to stimulate the conversation in a direction which will include the new arrival. Suitable comments might include: "George returned from a two-week vacation in Greece"; "Susan has recently been promoted to senior editor at Random House"; "David and Beth got engaged last week"; "Allison adopted a new kitten named Phoebe."

Suitable/Unsuitable Topics • When I was reared among the British aristocracy I was taught that it was vulgar during dinner parties to discuss money, religion, sex, or politics. Safe and suitable topics included travel, art, theatre, weather, horticulture, and horses. Although contemporary American society doesn't set such narrow conversational limits there are certain subjects that I still consider inappropriate or unsuitable for most occasions. Anyone who becomes absorbed in recounting the monetary details of their possessions immediately falls from my social graces. I have worked for multi-millionaires who began each dinner party by pointing to various items in the room and listing their price tags. Such an approach to socializing rarely stimulates conversation. The host should always keep an ear to the conversational winds, listening for subjects which may be offensive to particular guests. You are certainly within your rights to change any topic that you deem unsuitable for polite conversation.

Keep It Flowing • The secret to keeping the conversation flowing is to gather a mix of listeners and talkers, introverts and extroverts, stars and star-gazers (see "Guest Lists"). Including a few animated friends who have perfected the art of free-flowing conversation will ease your burden. If you feel the conversation is not focused or fun, try to introduce a harmless topic that will include everyone. Television, current events, movies and Madonna will usually stimulate any faltering conversation.

Include Everyone • If you have a small group engaged in a single topic of conversation be sure that everyone in the group is involved. If one of the guests hasn't spoken in ten minutes and appears to be obsessed with examining your CD collection, change the topic to one which will include the lost soul. Even if you have carefully assembled a guest list (taking into account individual preferences) there will be moments when the guests willingly disengage from the conversation. They may be engrossed in listening to what someone else has to say or tired after a long day's work; so I only change topics if they appear uncomfortable or left out.

Changing Subjects • It is not only your *right* but your *duty* as host to change the subject whenever you feel it is inappropriate for the occasion. The following subject-changing methods can also be used for deflecting the occasional argument or embarrassing moment:

1. Humor. *As subtly as possible interject a funny or clever comment into the discussion. If you do it right, your guests will laugh. Once you are the focus of the room, quickly change the subject. Humor is the best of all methods; it releases the tension created by an uncomfortable topic.*

2. Change the music. *Often a change in music will change the mood—and the subject. When guests feel the musical transition they may be more inclined to allow for a change in topic. If you choose a particularly controversial or popular album or artist you may be able to provoke a musical discussion in which everyone can safely participate.*

3. Seat the guests for dinner. *Very few people will carry the same conversation to the dinner table. Conversely, if you've reached the end of the meal, move the guests from the table back to the living room. Physical transitions usually allow for subtle conversational transitions.*

4. Distract the offending individual. *If a guest insists on discussing a particular subject you deem unsuitable, distract the offending individual. Show him (or her) a recent photograph, book or article which might be of interest; ask him to assist you in the kitchen or to refill the champagne glasses; tell the guest you cannot wait another moment to show him the newly purchased———(fill in the blank with painting, chair, stereo, wall paper, etc.) in another room. If necessary, speak to the individual in* *private, explaining your reluctance to promote a discussion of the particular topic.*

I have organized parties which lasted for hours but felt like minutes because the conversation was so alive. An animated exchange of ideas, humorous remarks and personal anecdotes can buoy the spirits of the most despondent guests and further invigorate the hearts and minds of the most enthusiastic.

Flowers

A party without flowers is like a church choir without its lead soprano: the remaining elements may produce a desirable result but its richness, beauty and harmony is noticeably diminished. *Never underestimate the seductive powers of fresh flowers.* A red rose in a bud vase on the bathroom vanity or a simple arrangement of tulips on a coffee table can elevate your guests' spirits by creating a warm, inviting and esthetically pleasing environment. They help transform anxious aunts into relaxed relatives and skeptical socialites into fond friends. Contrary to popular belief, you don't have to hire a florist or spend a small fortune on this integral entertaining element. Whenever I organize a party, I buy and arrange all of the flowers myself.

> **"Flowers are the poetry of reproduction. They are an example of the eternal seductiveness of life."**
>
> **—Jean Giraudoux**

◆ Floral considerations

Occasion • The purpose of the party should influence the type of flowers you present. For business functions I always create very simple arrangements (a grouping of tulips or roses placed in a beautiful crystal vase); for family and friends I add color and creativity to my choices. I always feel that the more celebratory the occasion—New Year's Eve, a twenty-fifth anniversary party or a fortieth birthday—the more wild and extravagant you can be with the floral arrangements.

Colors • Some hosts choose colors identical to the food they'll be serving or the clothes they'll be wearing; others try to match a particular hue in a painting or the overall decor of their home. I prefer white flowers (roses, lilies, orchids, tulips): living in an all-white apartment, I feel they enhance the drama of the space. Occasionally, I add a color accent for a particular holiday (red for Christmas) or just to give my guests something to talk about: they've become so used to my signature "white" that if, for any reason, I use a splash of color their curiosity is aroused. Color choices may be influenced by specific holidays—green for St. Patrick's Day, red-white-blue for the Fourth of July—but I don't recommend the use of dyed flowers. They have a cartoon-like appearance and lose their poetic quality when their natural color is so dramatically altered.

Size of the Table • Floral arrangements vary based upon the size and dimension of your dinner table. Round tables can accommodate floral arrangements with larger circumferances than rectangular tables. Flowers should never become an obstacle to socializing, transforming a three-course dinner into a game of peek-a-boo through the peonies. The beauty of round dining tables (unlike their rectangular counterparts) is that they provide dinner guests equal access to everyone seated at the table. Oversized centerpieces diminish this benefit (see "Centerpieces"). To safeguard against this social obstacle I recommend arranging the flowers and then sitting in each of the chairs, gaining the perspective of each guest. Remove or trim stems that inhibit anyone's ability to converse. With practice, you'll be able to gauge any obstructions by glancing at the table.

Budgets • The mark-up on flowers is between 200–400 percent. You can keep costs to a minimum, however, by purchasing flowers from your local flower market. In New York, I make most of my floral purchases at the 28th Street market where a bunch of French white tulips depletes only $18 from my entertaining budget. If bought at a retail florist, these same tulips could cost as much $75. Certain shops specialize in reasonably priced "day-old" flowers. If you're trying to save money, choose less expensive varieties such as freesia, daffodils, tulips and daisies; beware of the costly lilies, roses and orchids, which quickly add up. If you choose to use the services of a professional florist, shop around and get several price quotes.

Personal Preferences • Floral choices should be an extension of your style. While I can appreciate the magnificence of combining tiger lilies, ruben lilies, roses, delphiniums, liatras and poppies into a single arrangement, I prefer the simplicity of a dozen white tulips gracing an elegant crystal vase or a ceramic pot planted with paper whites. When I am creating arrangements for the dining table I stay clear of heavily scented flowers like freesias, lilies and paper whites that overwhelm one's sense of smell. For summer/outdoor entertaining I prefer multi-colored sweet peas whose soft, floppy petals rustle in the wind.

◆ Silk?

Under the appropriate circumstances, high-quality silk flowers can be a cost-effective alternative to fresh blossoms. Last year, after searching for months, I finally located beautiful silk philaenopsis orchid stems. Although the $25 per stem price may seem steep, it was a bargain compared to the $150 orchid plants I was replacing every 6–8 weeks on my coffee table. I purchased three silk stems and planted them in a white ceramic pot containing dried Spanish moss. For less than $100 I was able to create a beautiful arrangement that most guests mistake for the real thing. It doesn't produce the beautiful aroma of a living plant but as an orchid enthusiast it offered me a reasonable alternative. *If you buy silk flowers, always invest in the best.* Nothing looks worse than the inexpensive wrinkled variety.

I never use silk flowers on a dining room table. The distance between the guest and the flowers is not enough to maintain that "willing suspension of disbelief." Sitting down to a beautifully set table featuring artificial flowers is like being served a frozen dinner. Try to maintain a distance of at least three feet between your guests and anything artificial. And don't forget to periodically dust silk flowers and wash them once a year.

Fun Factor

Whether you're a secretary trying to survive the constant criticism of a tenacious task master or a harried host earnestly endeavoring to entertain a group of friends, finding the "fun factor" is as imperative as completing the task. It separates dizzying dread from anticipatory delight and transforms "I can't wait until it's over!" into "I can't wait to begin!" I'm fortunate; certain aspects of entertaining that many people find daunting were nothing more than childhood games I played with my sister. Being raised in an environment where dinner parties were a weekly occurrence helped me realize how entertaining "entertaining" can be.

◆ Defining the fun factor

"One man's fear is another man's fun." While some hosts might squirm at the thought of having to set the table for a three-course dinner for twelve, I welcome the opportunity. The prospect of combining an assortment of silver, china, linen and flowers to create a picture-perfect table setting is an irresistible invitation to play. The sense of "play" is at the heart of the fun factor: it is that aspect of entertain-

> **"No profit grows where there is no pleasure taken."**
> —Shakespeare,
> *The Taming of the Shrew*

ing that stimulates, excites and energizes the host. Parties provide the perfect excuse for playing chef, florist, disc jockey, comedian, songstress, talk-show host, model, bartender and anything else you can imagine. To find the fun factor, just define what you like or dislike about entertaining.

◆ Accentuate the positive

Once you decide what you like about entertaining, expand and accentuate that particular aspect. If you enjoy, as I do, creating beautiful and unique table settings, have fun experimenting with new approaches. If you are an enthusiastic chef, look upon a dinner party as a chance to exercise your culinary talents: rifle through all of your cookbooks (or buy some new ones) and find an exciting recipe that you would like to try. One of my friends is a record collector and amateur disc jockey; his main purpose in entertaining is to sample the new tapes he creates from his mammoth collection, mixing a variety of contemporary hits, legendary singers and obscure sounds. Focusing on what you enjoy will have a positive effect on your attitude for the overall function.

◆ Eliminate (or simplify) the negative

If you love socializing with friends in your home but hate to cook, either (a) have cocktail parties, (b) order take-out, (c) choose a very simple menu (pasta and salad), (d) purchase pre-cooked foods or (e) hire a caterer. Don't feel obligated to do anything you absolutely detest. If you're uncomfortable with large group entertaining, stick to small numbers. Some people find a group of sixteen for dinner overwhelming. But four groups of four on separate evenings is quite manageable. Try to remember that there is nothing written in stone that requires that you make specific choices or entertain in a particular style. The secret is in making choices that excite you. No matter how much *I* may love to fuss over a table setting, if *you* can't bear the thought of cleaning and setting a collection of silver, glass and china—offer a buffet.

◆ **Experimentation**

The next time you have to entertain a few close friends or relatives incorporate a new idea into the event. Experimentation is the best way to keep your entertaining style alive— but be wary of making bold new choices when entertaining business associates or acquaintances. These functions tend to be anxiety-producing.

Finding the fun-factor is an important exercise for anyone who extends an invitation. Whether it's a handful of relatives for your daughter's fifth birthday or forty business associates celebrating a successful venture, the organization and execution of parties should be a pleasurable experience—not an exercise in agony.

Guest Lists

Creating a guest list is like casting a play: based upon bits of background information, experience, and the perception of an individual's strengths and weaknesses, the host selects a variety of people whom he (or she) hopes will relate in such a manner so as to create an exciting evening of entertainment. Entertaining is about interacting; the guests' personalities can't help but influence the outcome. No matter how beautifully you set the table or how painstakingly you prepare the food, if the guest list is assembled without careful consideration, the results can be disastrous.

Many years ago I was invited by some family friends to attend a formal dinner party in London. Although the host and hostess were a courteous couple, they rarely spoke. Imagine my frustration when, on the occasion of my visit, I realized that they had surrounded themselves with similarly silent types. During the lengthy dinner my animated voice repeatedly interrupted pauses more pregnant than a woman about to give birth to triplets. No matter how many questions I asked or the diversity of topics I introduced, the con-

> **"Everyone has the potential to be an interesting and entertaining guest when placed in a comfortable environment amongst a group of people who share a common interest; it is the host's responsibility to establish the environment and define the group."**
>
> **—Michael Cherkinon**

versation rarely flowed for more than a few minutes. By the end of the evening I felt as if I had given a three-hour driving lesson to a group of students who never mastered the use of the clutch. The hostess failed to realize that she had mixed a group of "listeners" with only one "talker"—not the best combination unless you're attending a lecture or sitting in church.

◆ Guest list guidelines

Keep these suggestions in mind when preparing guest lists— no matter how small or large the occasion.

Invite People Whose Company You En-joy • While this may seem obvious I am constantly surprised by hosts who extend invitations to people they don't like just to fill out a dinner table. If you *have* to include someone for familial or business purposes, try to find something positive about the individual—a common interest, hobby or viewpoint you can share.

Invite People Who You Think Will Enjoy Each Other's Company • While I certainly do not advocate grouping people by profession (lawyers, bankers, writers, etc.) when making up a guest list, there should be areas of interest that overlap to allow for lively conversation. If you include someone whom you believe has nothing in common with the rest of the guests, that person may feel uncomfortable. Last fall I attended a dinner party honoring a friend of mine at one of New York's trendy discotheques. I was seated amid a group of "club kids": outrageously attired young

> **"There are no bad guests — just bad guest lists."**

adults between the ages of eighteen and twenty-two who sleep by day, party by night and purchase costumes and make-up in between. I'm certain the conversation was as straining for them as the ear-shattering techno-pop "dinner music" was for me. Although I made every possible effort to converse it soon became painfully apparent (to me at least) that the only "overlapping" which was going to occur was the contents of their wine glasses spilling onto my dinner plate.

Mix "Listeners" with "Talkers" • Most guests fall into two conversational categories: listeners—people who prefer listening and (hopefully) asking questions and responding to the general conversation; and talkers—those who are gregarious by nature, like to "take stage" and have no shortage of anecdotes or opinions on any number of subjects. A carefully prepared guest list should contain a balance of people from both categories. Too many listeners and the party becomes a one-man show (as was the case with my London dinner party); an abundance of talkers and the event turns into a vocal wrestling match.

Mix Regulars with Irregulars • Combining people you have previously entertained with first-time guests will help you to relax, and assure you of assembling a lively group. Reducing the guest list to a group of people who see each other regularly can reduce the sense of occasion as well as limit the conversational possibilities. Including new faces will stimulate the party by invigorating the regulars. Conversely, entertaining a group made up wholly of unfamiliar faces leaves a lot to chance. A few friends in the crowd will relax any host.

Try to Include an "Assistant" • If you're "hosting solo"—entertaining without the assistance of a spouse, loved one, or hired help—you may find it helpful to include a friend who can act as your second in command should the need arise. With larger groups, I try to include one or two close friends whom I feel comfortable calling upon to assist me with certain tasks (refilling wine or champagne glasses, clearing the table, overseeing accidents). Knowing there is "back-up" in such close proximity can be very comforting—especially when something unexpected happens.

Try to Include a Special or Surprise Guest • Inviting someone "special" will make your guests feel as if they are part of a unique occasion. Special guests might be: local celebrities or politicians; an out-of-town and much liked relative; a new love interest you've been talking about for weeks; someone you think would be the perfect match for one of your eternally single friends. Special guests create the feeling of "occasion" and focus the event. Be careful that your party doesn't become entirely about a single individual, however.

Guest Preferences

When entertaining "first-time guests" (those people whom you have never entertained in your home before) it is helpful to find out something about their preferences—especially regarding food. You'll not only flatter them with your research but you may prevent an awkward or embarrassing moment. There is nothing worse than slaving for hours in the kitchen to create bouillabaisse and a homemade berry pie only to find out that the guest of honor hates fish and is allergic to the walnuts in the pie crust. The combination of adventurous menus and cautious palates does not a successful dinner party make. A few well-placed phone calls and inquiries will ensure that your entertaining efforts are rewarded.

◆ Who to ask?

Most first-time guests fall into one of the following categories: relatives, friends of friends, business associates or co-workers. Whenever I attempt to uncover my guests' likes and dislikes I prefer not to ask them directly. I question friends, relatives, or co-workers, explaining the circumstances. You'll find that the individuals you question are so taken with your initiative that they offer wonderful details which can be incorporated into the event. If you're nervous about entertaining your future in-laws for the first time, surprise them with their favorite red wine or blend of coffee. When they realize you've made an effort to find out something about their preferences you'll make them feel special, which will certainly help to alleviate their (and your) anxiety. One of the secrets of successful entertaining is an ability to make *each* guest feel special.

◆ What to ask?

The following list provides an overview of the type of questions to ask. You shouldn't feel compelled, however, to fill out a detailed "questionnaire" on each individual. The extent to which you try to find out background information on your guests will be influenced by the particular occasion and the impression you are trying to create.

Food Preferences

- *What type of food does the guest love?*

- *Is there a particular food the guest hates?*

- *Is the guest allergic to any particular foods?*

- *Is the guest on any particular diet (vegetarian, fat-free, macrobiotic, low-cholesterol)?*

- *Does the guest have any religious beliefs that might prevent him or her from eating certain foods*

(Jewish friends who are strictly Kosher, Catholics who do not eat meat on Friday, etc.)?

Alcohol Preferences

● Does the guest have a favorite champagne, wine, or liquor?

● Does the guest drink? If not, respect his or her choice and find suitable substitutes. I once attended a Manhattan dinner party where the overly enthusiastic host insisted each of his guests have a shot of iced vodka following dinner. Although one soft-spoken gentleman repeatedly declined, the host was relentless. What the host did not know was that the guest had completed an alcohol rehabilitation program two weeks prior. With such unyielding encouragement to imbibe the "recovered" alcoholic was soon sliding down the slopes of sobriety: he began singing Broadway melodies louder than Ethel Merman in the last act of Gypsy. Never force anything on anyone.

Pets

● Is the guest allergic to any pets?

● Does the guest have a fear of the animal you allow to roam throughout your home? Most hosts can appreciate the fact that the majority of their guests might not warm to a friendly boa constrictor slithering across the living room floor but fail to understand that certain people are truly frightened by cats and dogs. Do not use a dinner party as an opportunity to help a guest overcome fears. Respect the individual's feelings and keep the pet in another room. (See "Pets.")

● Does the guest have a pet (such as a dog) which might become an unexpected guest at your dining table? Certain celebrities are known for traveling with their pets in hand (or bag, as the case may be). I believe Spike Rivers (Joan Rivers's adorable Yorkshire Terrier) attended more socially signifi-cant parties last year than I did. If you have reason to believe that you might become the recipient of an unexpected four-legged guest, speak to the proud pet owner before the event.

Smoker
Non-smoker

● Does the guest smoke? If so and you have a smoke-free home decide how you wish to handle the situation. (See "Smoking.")

● Is the guest allergic to smoke? If so and you allow smoking in your home decide how you wish to handle the situation. Ask the smokers if, in light of the guest's allergies, they would mind smoking in another room or outdoors.

Flowers

- *Does the guest have a favorite flower? For romantic dinners, birthday celebrations and anniversaries, a table that is set with your special guest's favorite flowers will certainly steer the evening in the right direction.*

- *Is the guest allergic to any particular flower?*

Music

- *Does the guest prefer—or dislike—any particular style of music?*

- *Does the guest have a favorite singer or group? (See "Music.")*

Discovering information about your guests' preferences should not be an exhaustive and time-consuming mission. Remember that you are a host who is in the process of organizing a party—not a CIA agent about to uncover a breach in national security. A little research, however, will enable you to make choices that will benefit both you and your guests.

Inebriated Guests

Entertaining guests is like being in charge of the roller coaster at an amusement park: although you hope that everyone has an exhilarating experience you must also enforce those rules that ensure that everyone has a safe ride. When guests pass through your front door they are, in essence, entrusting themselves to your care—even to the extent that you might have to protect them from themselves. Everyone who entertains must have an unwritten set of rules regarding alcohol consumption. And every host should not be intimidated by or feel uncomfortable about enforcing those rules.

◆ Ways to prevent guests from exceeding their limit

1. One of the reasons I serve champagne exclusively (see "Champagne") is that it simplifies the process of tracking the amount of alcohol being served (count how many bottles you've served and in what amount of time). If you offer a variety of mixed drinks make mental notes throughout the luncheon or dinner. If you notice that a full bottle of Scotch is half empty an hour into your party and only one guest is drinking Scotch, investigate the situation.

2. Always serve food with alcohol. Even if you're organizing a brief cocktail party before going on to another location, have a variety of snacks or hors d'oeuvre on hand.

3. If you think someone is reaching his (or her) limit, don't offer another drink—wait until the person asks. Remember that you are in control of the speed at which drinks are refilled, so slow down the process, if necessary.

4. If you feel someone has reached the limit but insists on another drink, try substituting with watered down drinks, water, juice or virgin blender drinks. If the person notices, apologetically inform the thirsty soul that you are running low on a particular type of alcohol; thank the guest for understanding your need to stretch out the supplies.

5. If the climate and/or occasion permits, walk the guest near an open window or terrace for a breath of fresh air or suggest a stroll around the block.

6. If you are having a cocktail hour before dinner and someone is exceeding his limit, cut the cocktail hour short and seat your guests.

◆ **Early signals that a guest may be reaching his or her limit**

1. Uncharacteristic behavior: shy friends who begin to act extremely extroverted; articulate individuals who begin rambling.

2. *Mood swings.*

3. *A noticeable change in posture.*

4. Speaking at a volume inappropriate for the space.

5. Lack of basic motor skills.

6. Inappropriate behavior.

WHAT TO DO

1. Cut off the supply of alcohol in a subtle manner. If possible, substitute with non-alcoholic beverages. If the guest creates a fuss, act the part of the overly concerned mother who is only trying to take care of her favorite child.

2. If the guest feels ill, escort him to a private room; place a cool towel on his forehead and let him lie down for awhile. If your duties as host do not permit you to leave the party, ask your spouse or a close friend to assist you.

3. If the guest becomes belligerent take immediate action; help him to a safe but swift departure. Call a cab or car service, or ask a friend to drive the person home. Escort the inebriated guest directly into the cab or car to ensure that he does not have an accident along the way. If necessary, tip the cab driver and ask him to escort your guest to the front door.

4. Do not attempt to engage in a discussion about alcohol consumption (or anything else). If the intoxicated person does not comply with your polite requests, be firm. In no way allow him to intimidate you or make you feel as if you are behaving in a rude manner.

> If you are, in any way, uncertain about your guests' ability to drive safely, don't let them get behind the wheel. It is better to risk offending a guest than contributing to his death by not taking action.

◆ Guests who drive

One of the greatest advantages of living in a city like Manhattan is that you can drink at parties without worrying about driving home. Although there is an ever increasing awareness about the subject, some people still do not realize that drinking and driving is a lethal combination. You don't have to look very far before you find friends and relatives whose lives have been irrevocably altered by someone who exceeds his limit and sits behind the wheel of a car. The mother of the co-author of this book was killed by a drunk driver. The papers are filled with tragic tales that can be traced to an abuse of alcohol. It is a problem that affects everyone. In certain states a host can be held legally responsible for the hazardous behavior of his legally intoxicated guests.

I always make a point of finding out which of my guests will be driving home; throughout the evening I scrutinize the alcohol consumption of this particular group. If one of my driving guests has exceeded his limit I either (a) call a cab or car service, (b) ask a friend to drive, (c) drive the person myself, (d) let the guest sleep in my apartment, or (e) make arrangements for the guest to sleep in a nearby motel or hotel.

◆ Hosts who drink

If, as host, you are going to be monitoring the alcohol consumption of your guests you must, first, monitor your own consumption. I don't believe that a host must forsake his glass of champagne but he must limit his intake. In addition to continually keeping an eye on the guests' alcohol consumption, a host must juggle several duties throughout the party. Excessive alcohol consumption will put you at a disadvantage, leading to sloppy entertaining. If you are entertaining with someone I advocate naming a "Designated Host": as with designated drivers, this person will ultimately be responsible for monitoring and overseeing the entire event. The designated host must *never* approach, let alone exceed, his limit.

There is no other area of entertaining which so dramatically affects not only the lives of the people you are entertaining, but the lives of strangers (for whom you are equally responsible). Each time you open your front door to a group of friends and pour them a drink you must embrace the responsibility with a clear head and a scrutinizing eye.

Intervening Entities

They masquerade as the most benevolent creatures: well-meaning mothers-in-law intent upon spicing up your spaghetti sauce; over-affectionate aunts adamant about stacking the Steuben in the dishwasher; frugal fathers who haunt your home by turning out lights in unoccupied rooms. Everyone has encountered overzealous relatives and guests who try to "lessen your load." As host it is your job to decide whether or not you need their assistance or politely decline the offer without offending anyone.

> "With intervening entities, just smile and say, 'No thank you . . . *please!*' "
>
> **—Emma Louise Cross**

Certain hosts accept help they don't want because they do not know how to say "No." Allowing someone to assist with tasks with which they may not be familiar increases the risk of something going wrong. Some of the mishaps I have witnessed during my many years of party-giving and going include:

- *The kind-hearted sister-in-law who offered to make the coffee but wouldn't take "no" for an answer even though she was not familiar with the particular coffee maker: Her efforts resulted in a muddy river flowing across the kitchen counter, into the drawers and onto the floor.*

● *The twelve-year-old son of a multi-millionaire Hollywood producer who insisted on refilling the champagne glasses at a garden party: He splashed over half a bottle of Dom Perignon across some of the entertainment industry's most powerful laps.*

● *The slightly "tipsy" guest who felt the room was too stuffy: He opened a broken window which was held together by a single sash, awaiting the repair-man. The glass frame smashed and fell fifteen flights down to the street below. The incoming rush of 8-degree winter air helped cool off the room and put a quick end to the party.*

The most important thing to remember when dealing with intervening entities is: *Be gracious but firm in maintaining control of your party and your home.*

◆ **How to refuse help without appearing rude**

Remind Your Guests That It Is Your Pleasure to Wait on Them ● Tell your well-meaning friends that part of the joy you derive from entertaining is being able to care for their every comfort. When you are a guest in *their* home, *they* can reciprocate in a like manner.

Explain That Because Your Kitchen Is Small You Have to Be Overly Organized • Their assistance, although well-intended, would only confuse you. This excuse is actually quite close to the truth but it makes it appear as if they are assisting you by *not* doing anything.

Distract the Intervening Entity •

1. Introduce a volatile topic of conversation which you know will interest the individual. Provocative subjects include: politics, the Royal Family, and Elizabeth Taylor.

2. Introduce the individual to a guest whom they haven't previously met and ask them to recount the hilarious story about the time they . . .

3. Show the individual a family photo, magazine article or the new carpeting in the guest bedroom.

If All Else Fails • Give the person a small task which will allow him or her to feel helpful but will not interfere with the execution of your affair. Suitable tasks include:

1. Ask the guest to "make the rounds" and see if anyone needs anything. This will often divert the person into a conversation with your other guests.

2. Ask the helpful creature to walk your dog; if you don't have a dog—don't let the guest know. This will distract your guest for at least an hour.

3. Tell the intervening entity that the party cannot

*continue until your albums, cassettes and CDs are
alphabetized by the artist's last name.*

When dealing with intervening entities it is important to be
as diplomatic as possible in declining help. You do not want
guests to feel rejected when you do not enthusiastically embrace their offer of assistance. As David Frost once said,
"Diplomacy is the art of letting somebody else have your
way."

Intimidation Factor

The only thing you have to fear is*:

a. *making a fool of yourself*

b. *your mother-in-law's nagging criticism*

c. *fear itself*

For many of my friends, the thought of organizing a sit-down dinner for eight is an impossible dream. Although they'd love to be able to reciprocate the type of hospitality I extend whenever I entertain in my home, most of my friends profess "entertaining ignorance" and have an unconquerable fear of embarrassing themselves.

It can be extremely frustrating if you're a socially spirited individual but weren't raised in an environment in which party planning was an everyday occurrence. The choices to be made and the obstacles to be overcome may seem overwhelming. Although I always try to discourage such anxiety a few of my friends worry that I (or anyone who entertains regularly) will scrutinize their entertaining efforts and offer a verbal report card throughout the evening. You shouldn't allow such fears to inhibit you from sharing your home with friends, relatives, and business associates. Entertaining is not

*The correct answer is c: "fear itself."

all about food. It's about creating an environment in which you and your guests can relax in a manner which allows something new to be shared. The most glorious four-star restaurants of the world cannot compare with what *you* have to offer when entertaining in your home.

◆ How to overcome the intimidation factor

Start Slow • If you don't have a lot of experience in party planning don't begin by organizing a formal sit-down dinner for twelve important business associates. A luncheon or Sunday brunch is an excellent beginning. Daytime functions are usually more casual, the atmosphere more relaxing. You will feel less pressured to have to perform.

Plan a Simple Menu • Don't be overly ambitious your first time out of the "cooking gate." Just because you have extended a dinner invitation doesn't mean you have to start searching through every cookbook ever printed for some exotic recipe. And no matter how much you would like to make an impression on your guests, don't try to duplicate the complete menu from *Babette's Feast* or the hand spun caramelized sugar baskets filled with white chocolate mousse and raspberry sauce that you saw last week on a French cooking show. Choose recipes that (a) you have made before, (b) you enjoy preparing, and, (c) do not require hours of preparation.

Prepare • If you are the type of person who gets anxious at the thought of entertaining, prepare as much as you can in advance. This will free you up during the actual function so that you aren't cross-referencing six different lists, trying to remember what to do next. Plan a menu that can be made in advance and reheated (stews, casseroles, lasagna). The day before, set the table, select the wine, serving utensils, and serving platters that you will be using. The more you accomplish before the party the more in control you will begin to feel.

Rehearse • Write a schedule of everything you need to do once your guests have arrived; review the schedule several times in your head until it becomes a logical sequence of events, one activity leading to the next. If it would make you feel more comfortable, set the table and practice clearing (see "Serving & Clearing the Table"). Walk through your schedule in the kitchen to familiarize yourself with the sequence. You can never be over-rehearsed in the mechanics of entertaining.

Don't Expect Perfection • As with any newly acquired skill, entertaining without fear takes time and practice. Don't judge yourself if something goes wrong. Remind yourself that everyone has to start somewhere; it's not a "life or death" matter. Look upon the mishap as a dear old friend who pays an occasional visit. Make light of whatever goes wrong and keep moving forward.

Take Pride in Your Home • Don't allow yourself to be intimidated or embarrassed by guests who may live or entertain in a more extravagant style than yourself. And don't try to compete. Remember that successful entertaining is about making choices that reflect who *you* are—not who your guests are.

Look upon the Experience as an Adventure • Entertaining is like riding "Space Mountain" at Disneyworld: a sometimes anxious but always exhilarating experience which, with its "ups and downs," is filled with laughter, excitement and, on occasion, a few screams. Your attitude will affect the outcome of the event.

If you make the effort to take that first plunge into the sometimes choppy and challenging waters of party-planning, you will soon discover the joy of filling your home with the sounds of stimulating conversation and laughter offered by loving friends and relatives.

Invitations

A properly executed invitation is like a preview to an eagerly anticipated film: providing more than just the essential information (who, what, when, where and why) it evokes an emotion or idea that characterizes the event. If done with a sense of style, purpose, creativity and wit, an invitation will elicit an enthusiastic "I can't wait! I have to to be a part of that!" response. Whenever I'm planning a party I choose one or two adjectives that describe the feeling I want to create (playful, graceful, elegant, outrageous, whimsical); I then make choices about everything from the invitations and the menu to the table setting and music which enhance the particular feeling.

Implement the following suggestions to create "previews" to what are destined to be "blockbuster" events.

◆ **Timing**

Deciding when to issue an invitation varies on the particular function. Formal celebrations and special occasions (weddings, cotillions, anniversary and retirement parties) require at least six weeks' notice to ensure that the guests have not already committed themselves to another social engagement. Small gatherings of business associates or friends should be notified at least two weeks prior to the event; informal parties can be organized a few days or even a few hours ahead of time. I always allow longer lead times when mailing invitations to other states or foreign cities.

◆ Types of invitations

In social days past a beautifully inscribed card "Requesting Your Presence" was the only acceptable form of invitation for noteworthy occasions. The contemporary approach to guest-gathering is less formal and more spontaneous. Taking into consideration the type of event you are planning (dinner party, brunch, cocktail party, surprise birthday) any of the following types of invitations (under the appropriate circumstances) are acceptable:

Written • Unless you are a calligrapher with hours of free time, handwritten invitations are no longer practical. As a child, I used to flip through a photo album filled with numerous handwritten invitations my family had received throughout the year. With closed eyes, I would brush my finger tips across each perfectly inscribed card and imagine myself instantly transported into the designated ballrooms, stately mansions, castles, and country estates. If you have the skill and the patience, or can afford to hire a professional calligrapher (they can charge up to $10 per invite), handwritten invitations offer a very special preview to very elegant affairs.

Store Bought • Fill in the necessary information, place the cards in the accompanying envelopes and they're ready to be mailed. Anyone with a busy schedule can appreciate the ease of inviting twenty-five guests to a birthday party in thirty minutes or less. What you save in time, however, you sacrifice in originality. If your your schedule allows, I recommend a more creative approach.

Engraved • Weddings are still the most popular occasion for professionally engraved invitations that evoke a sense of formality. They're also suitable for engagement parties and very special large group events. For smaller functions—a dinner party for eight—engraved invitations can appear pretentious.

Computer Generated • Certain computer software packages (Microsoft's Windows) offer very sophisticated options for creating invitations. With a variety of fonts, graphics and colors from which to choose, it's like having a print shop in your own home. If you have the aptitude and the equipment, computer-generated invitations offer a wonderful opportunity for creating something original.

Telephone • I extend the majority of my invitations for small gatherings via the telephone. For informal events, I prefer the immediate and personal approach of verbally inviting someone into my home. If no one answers, it is perfectly acceptable to leave an invitation on an answering machine. In such instances, relate all of the necessary information; ask the individual to ring back so that you can make a personal connection and provide additional details.

Fax • Faxed invitations are becoming more popular for business entertaining. They (a) get there immediately, (b) save you the time of addressing envelopes, (c) save the recipient the time of taking or returning a phone call, and (d) are inexpensive. Because everyone does not yet own a fax machine (can it be far behind personal computers, compact disc players and VCRs?), I rarely use faxed invitations for social entertaining.

Creative and Unique • Create an unusual invitation that is representative of the feeling or spirit of the event. For birthday parties or anniversaries use photographs of the individual or couple with the necessary information on the back. Two years ago I received an invitation to a Halloween party that requested that the guests dress as old screen legends. The invitation was fashioned after the screen of Grauman's Chinese Theatre in Hollywood. As you slid a tab across the bottom of the invitation, the necessary party information moved across the screen.

Individually created invitations *can* get out of hand. One particularly affluent Fifth Avenue society matron created quite a social stir when she had custom-made jeweled bags containing invitations hand-delivered by her chauffeur. Regardless of her motives, many of the guests felt as if they were being purchased for the evening. Invitations can be exotic but should never be ostentatious.

◆ **Reminders**

1. I always follow-up my invitations with a telephone call, reminding the guest of the event and confirming that the individual will attend. For long-term invitations I telephone the week before; for short-term, a day or two before is acceptable. If you are organizing a formal event or large party I recommend mailing a "reminder" card a week before which states, "Mr. and Mrs. Oliver Smith look forward to your company on Saturday, December 18th at 8 P.M."

2. Always let your guests know if there is a proposed dress code. This will save you and your guests any embarrassing moments. I once attended a Saturday night poolside barbecue in Los Angeles. One of the female guests had either confused the dates or neglected to read the invitation: she arrived in a beaded evening dress accessorized with long white gloves.

3. If you are hosting a birthday, anniversary or retirement party and do not want your guests to feel obligated to bring a gift, simply state "No Gifts, Please" on the invitations. It would not be considered rude, however, if, as a guest, you ignored the request.

4. Prepare your invitations and issue them all at one time. This ensures that friends, relatives or business associates do not feel slighted—like "second-string" guests—if they receive their invitations a week later than everyone else. In spite of your best efforts, the mail can still play havoc with your invitations.

If what William Hazlitt once wrote is true—"the best part of our lives we pass in counting on what is to come"—then an invitation should be created in a fascinating and fantastical manner to ensure that each recipient is aroused with the greatest of expectations.

Kitchens

Although often unseen, the kitchen is the heart and soul of any entertaining event. Everything from food to forks passes through its portals, transforming a collection of glasses and guests into a spirited social occasion. Just as a malfunctioning heart will affect the performance of the entire body, a disorganized kitchen can't help but hinder the health of a lively dinner party. It can sometimes be painfully apparent if the host is not in control of the kitchen. Clues include: the sounds of crystal crashing and cutlery clattering onto the kitchen floor; a lapse of (what feels like) hours between the courses; dessert plates that feature edges randomly decorated with bits of mashed potatoes; curious kitchen noises punctuated by human cries; a slightly smoky odor followed by the host calmly asking, "Does anyone have a fire extinguisher?"

The following considerations will help organize any kitchen, ensuring that your next dinner party does not suffer the consequences of a malfunctioning heart.

◆ Before a party

Refrigerator • Clean, stock and organize the refrigerator with all the necessary party items. Divide the refrigerator into sections, placing the beer, wine or champagne in one area, specific food items in another. Organizing the refrigerator in this manner ensures that you won't have to search its entire contents, trying to find the salad dressing or another bottle of wine. Never store dinner party provisions on the back shelf where they are easily lost or forgotten. Whenever possible, prepare and stack plates in the refrigerator. If I serve salad, cold entrees or desserts, I prepare the individual plates ahead of time and arrange them in a designated area of my refrigerator. When I'm ready to serve each course, I remove the required plates, add the necessary salad dressing or garnish, and serve. It's a great time-saving method that enables you to spend more time with your guests.

Stove • If you don't start with a clean stove top and/or oven you increase (a) the work at the end of the event and (b) the possibility of unintentionally altering food tastes. It is embarrassing to grill salmon and then discover (at the dinner table) that the flavor has been altered by the grease droppings from last week's lamb roast. Organize the stove-top burners, deciding ahead of time which pots and pans will be used and on which specific burners. If you need to bake and broil (potatoes and fish, for example), decide upon a cooking sequence that won't interfere with the timing of the meal.

Counter Tops • All counter spaces should be thoroughly cleaned and cleared before the party begins. Set out the plates, serving platters and utensils that you will be using. Cluttered counter tops create chaos in the kitchen and anxiety in the host.

Dishwasher • Run the dishwasher and empty its contents before the guests arrive. This allows maximum space for stacking when the table is cleared (see "Cleaning Up" and "Serving & Clearing the Table.")

Garbage • Empty all garbage cans ahead of time. There is enough to keep you busy during a party without having to worry about emptying or changing trash bin liners.

Sinks • Sinks should be emptied and scrubbed. If you start with a full sink you have no room to maneuver. This leads to cluttered counter tops which triggers a chain reaction of moving and maneuvering various items. When you're pressed for time and trying to locate a serving knife or soup ladle you'll find yourself performing pivots faster than a basketball player.

◆ **During a party**

Organization • Maintaining an organized kitchen is key to any successful dinner party. If you've organized the cooking area ahead of time, working through the courses should be effortless. Don't abandon your commitment to an organized kitchen, however, when something goes wrong. Remind yourself that maintaining an ordered environment will assist you in overcoming any kitchen crisis. If you use a bottle opener or corkscrew place it in a designated spot so that it doesn't take five minutes to find it buried under the salad plates in the sink.

Clean As You Go • Without spending more than a few minutes away from your guests, clean counter tops, soak pans, and rinse and stack dishes as you work your way through a dinner party (see "Serving and Clearing the Table"). If you spill and/or drop anything, wipe and clean immediately. The amount of time it takes is worth avoiding the potential hazards created by broken china, glass, and spilt liquids and food. When cleaning, I recommend the use of paper towels over cloth. Although the cotton and linen varieties are decorative they can become unhygenic if improperly used. If you prefer cloth towels, use a freshly laundered set for each new function.

Quiet Kitchens • A professionally run kitchen should be "noise-free." There is nothing more disconcerting to dinner party conversation than the sounds of dishwashers rattling, plates clattering or cutlery carelessly tossed into a stainless steel sink. Unless your kitchen is located behind a sound-proof door (referred to as a "green door" in formal households) or hidden in a remote part of your home, be aware of the noise level you create when working. Remember, although you may not be seen in the kitchen, you certainly can be heard.

If you follow the preceding suggestions in creating and maintaining a clean, organized kitchen, the process of restoring your cooking area to its original order is relatively painless: repeat each of the steps outlined in "Before a Party." If, however, you have opted for a more spontaneous and haphazard approach, the challenge can be quite daunting. Although I am an advocate of everyone developing his or her own style, I have never attended a party where a host's disorganized approach and/or lack of control in the kitchen produced a more entertaining evening. Commanding your kitchen is a craft that will produce immeasurable rewards for both you and your guests.

Lighting

Lighting, like fine wine or good music, is one of the elements a host uses to seduce the resistant guest; it can transform a restless relative into a calm caller or an anxious acquaintance into a fond friend. Installing a dimmer switch on a dining-room chandelier or a glare-resistant light bulb in a living room lamp are inexpensive ways of creating a warm, relaxed, and inviting atmosphere.

Many hosts fail to realize that lighting choices can be as important as menu selection. Last winter I attended a holiday dinner party given by a friend of mine in Manhattan. She had set a magnificent table in the formal dining room of her spacious Upper West Side apartment. Unfortunately, the only source of light was a massive crystal chandelier that had not been placed on a dimmer. It produced such intense light that I noticed the dinner guests squint as they entered the room. The ladies present (who had obviously anticipated evening lighting) looked overly made-up and were visibly uncomfortable. The heads of two balding gentlemen seated across from me resembled a pair of head lights as they reflected the results of the overhead fixture. Unfortunately, the hostess was completely unaware of her ill-conceived illumination; no matter how hard she tried, the conversation rarely flowed; the guests could not wait to flee the room.

The following lighting considerations will enable any host to create an atmosphere in which a guest can relax, linger and enjoy the event:

◆ Light views

Too Bright? • A brightly lit room (especially for evening entertaining) is not conducive to successful socialization. Harsh lighting creates an environment where a guest feels exposed or "on display"; it doesn't encourage the type of intimate exchanges that transform a party into something special. Examine the placement of lighting fixtures in your entertaining space and the wattage of the light bulbs. Whenever possible, use three-way bulbs and/or dimmer switches that allow for various lighting combinations. If you prefer brightly lit rooms for everyday use, change the light bulbs for your party and replace them the next day.

Too Dark? • As a general rule, if you have to struggle to read your watch, the room is too dark. I've attended dinner parties where guests knocked over glasses or bumped into tables because the rooms were poorly lit. When creating a seductive atmosphere make sure that your choices do not create safety hazards. Take into account those visitors who are not familiar with your home and the positioning of furniture. I learned this lesson the hard way. My living room features a large glass oval-shaped coffee table which is cut in half with a three-inch gap separating the pieces. I organized a cocktail party one evening for several acquaintances. Because the room was not sufficiently lit one of my first-time guests did not realize that the glass table was in two pieces; she placed a champagne flute on what she thought was a glass surface but was actually the gap between the table halves. Imagine her surprise when she heard glass shattering on the floor. After that unfortunate mishap I readjusted the lighting in the room.

Dimmers • To provide the maximum flexibility in home lighting *all* fixtures should be placed on dimmers, including bathrooms and kitchens. The cost difference between regular ("on" and "off") and dimmer switches is just a few dollars; the investment is well worth the results. During certain parties I reduce the intensity of the lighting as the evening unfolds and my guests begin to relax. If done gradually, your guests may never realize that the lighting has been altered.

Flattering to Women • The most common culprits are harsh overhead lights, bright bulbs and odd color choices. Most women apply their evening make-up anticipating subdued lighting. Many have special make-up mirrors with various light adjustments to allow for such considerations. If your living or dining room is brightly lit a woman may look overly made up—as if she were about to walk onto a stage or into an undesirable profession.

Glare-free • If you own the type of lamps or lighting fixtures that allow for exposed light sources use glare-free (or frosted) bulbs. Position or angle the fixtures and shades to minimize the potential for a guest being blinded by a naked bulb. I always set the lights in my home for a particular function and then gradually move through the space, sitting in the various couches and chairs, examining the lighting. If

I find the tilt of a lamp prevents me from speaking to someone without squinting I make an adjustment. The more frequently you entertain the more familiar you will become with the potential lighting problems of your home.

Colors • Although most people associate light with something white, traditional light bulbs produce a yellow glow. Depending on your decor, this may or may not be desirable. Because I live in an all-white apartment traditional bulbs cast a yellowish tint on everything from walls to furniture, making it appear as my home was rapidly aging. After a great deal of research I located a Finnish-made bulb (Chromolux) that produces pure white light. I find the higher price of the bulbs (approximately $5 per bulb) worth the investment: They enhance not only the beauty of my home but the complexions of my visitors. Many of my female guests have remarked that my lighting was particularly flattering to their faces. I attribute much of the success to the discovery of this wonderful new light source. Be careful of how you use either fluorescent or neon lights which can be overpowering.

Candle Light • Candles mixed with indirect lighting create a wonderfully seductive atmosphere. Make sure they do not present a safety hazard and are not positioned at eye level: a glaring flame is very distracting. Candles work best in small, intimate spaces such as on a dinner table or bathroom vanity (see "Candles").

Lingerers

These menacing creatures disguise themselves in a variety of shapes and sizes: the enthusiastic cousin from Iowa who wants to reminisce, week by week, about the highlights of your high school years; the next-door neighbor who decides to stay "just one more hour" because "it only takes a minute to get home"; the office acquaintance who sinks back into the sofa, realizing that you're everything he ever wanted in a therapist. Maintaining your persona of "The Hospitable Host" when all you can think about is "getting the guest to go" is a formidable challenge which requires a plan, a little patience and a lot of diplomacy.

◆ Deciding when you've had enough

Most hosts know when they've fulfilled their duties and are ready to call it a day. For me, it's that moment when I realize that one of my guests is vividly recounting a near-death experience and all I can focus on is clearing, cleaning, and collapsing under the covers. If you are part of an "entertaining couple," however, the situation is more complicated: you and your loved one's SSL ("Social Satiation

> **"My evening visitors, if they cannot see the clock, should find the time in my face."**
>
> **—Emerson**

Level") may not be the same. In order to avoid an awkward or embarrassing moment, agree ahead of time on a signal which will indicate that "it's time for them to go!" Be warned: Unless you are capable of executing the signal with the subtle proficiency of an ex-Interpol agent, don't do it: find another way of communicating with your spouse which will not risk offending a guest.

◆ Suitable signals for couples

1. Ask your spouse to "look in on the children." (Of course, if you don't have children this may tip off your guests that you're trying to get rid of them.)

2. Remove or change the position of a piece of jewelry: take off a ring, watch or an earring—if someone notices, tell them the particular item was pinching your finger, wrist or ear.

3. Find a way to compliment your loved one; cap the compliment with a kiss on the cheek. Again, if affectionate behavior is not characteristic for your relationship, your guests might wonder what's going on.

4. Change the music to a particular "parting" song. Choose a tune with innocuous lyrics—not something as obvious as "The Party's Over" or Donna Summer's "Last Dance."

5. Beware of exchanging "The Look": glaring eyeball-to-eyeball contact accompanied by lowered eyebrows and pursed lips. In most instances, your guests will notice. The proficient host rises to the challenge of indicating fatigue in the subtlest way possible. I'm almost embarrassed to admit the number of parties I've attended where one of the hosts actually fell asleep while the party was still going on.

◆ The polite push

Thankfully, most people have a sense of when to leave. If, however, one of your guests appears to have traveled into a foreign time zone without a return ticket, try to determine what is preventing him from realizing that you would like to get on with your life. Without appearing rude or inhospitable, experiment with the following suggestions that should help to politely push any lingering types out the door.

Conversation • Let the conversational level gradually subside. Don't feel obligated to keep the dialogue moving. Allow what Chekhov described as an "angel of silence" to pass over the room.

Drinks • Don't refill glasses at the same pace which you did earlier in the evening. If you like, stop serving alcohol at a designated hour. Certain people may linger because they like the taste of your champagne. Apologize for "running out" and switch to coffee (decaffeinated, of course) or herbal tea.

Lights • If your lights are on dimmers, increase the level of illumination ever so slightly when the guest is out of the room. By altering the atmosphere you might be able to alter the individual's feelings about remaining.

Music • Change the music to something low key to lessen the energy level of the room. If you're playing an album and you notice that your lingering guest (with closed eyes and a bobbing head) is perfectly lip-synching every syllable of every song, you may want to change the album at an appropriate moment.

Don't Say "No" • Sometimes a guest is legitimately uncertain about whether or not he (or she) is overstaying his welcome. In such cases, the polite individual will say, "It's late. I should go." If you really want the guest to leave, don't say, "No." Acknowledge the fact that you had lost track of time because you were enjoying the company; make a polite excuse about why you have to get up early in the morning (doctor's appointment, work-related, driving someone to the airport). In most instances, you will be able to tell when an individual's departure hinges on your response.

As host, it is your responsibility to *politely* deal with the awkward situation of lingering guests. It is unfair to both you and your guest if you allow a perfectly lovely party to be ruined by not taking control of the situation. Decide upon a plan and implement it as discreetly as possible to ensure that "Some Enchanted Evening" doesn't turn into a nightmarish version of "The Guest That Wouldn't Go Away."

Menu Planning

Creating a menu that is innovative, tantalizing and affordable—and doesn't require weeks of preparation by a Cordon Bleu chef—can be challenging. But if you rise to the occasion armed with a few family recipes, an adventurous spirit—and a portable television in the kitchen—you might find yourself pleasantly surprised by the amount of fun you can have. During my three decades of party-planning I have organized and executed thousands of menus—some in conjunction with a fully trained staff (when I worked for very wealthy employers) but many by myself (whenever I entertain in my home).

> **Ode to a Waffling Chef**
>
> **Soup or salad? Beef or chicken? Menu planning Needn't be Grief stricken**
>
> **—anonymous**

Entertaining on a limited budget is sometimes easier because it narrows the field of culinary choices. I have wasted countless hours with employers who agonized for days, convinced that the success or failure of a dinner party hinged on whether the menu featured Beef carbonnades à la falmande, Chicken Vallé d'Auge or Veal à la Milanaise. If, however, you have four people to feed on a $25 budget, your options quickly come into focus. Although budgets are of primary importance when planning a menu there are other relevant factors to consider before making your choices.

◆ Menu planning considerations

The next time you face the formidable task of tantalizing your guests with gastronomical delights, considers the following:

Budgets • Obviously you cannot begin to plan a menu until you set a specific food budget. (See "Budgets.")

Time Restraints • Be realistic about what you can accomplish based on your other commitments and responsibilities. If you're a working mother with children and have decided to entertain on a week night, plan a menu that requires a minimal amount of preparation on the day of the event. If you're comfortable with the idea, buy prepared or take-out foods from local shops and restaurants. If your menu requires a considerable amount of attention during the party ask yourself if your absence will detract from the occasion. Never make choices that require you stay up the night before until 3 A.M.: A haggard host is not a happy host.

Size of the Event • Unless you're hiring a caterer, the simplicity of the menu should increase in direct proportion to the size of the event: the larger the group, the simpler the menu. I might prepare filet of sole stuffed with crab for a group of four but if the group expanded to eight I would switch to stews and casseroles, which require little last-minute preparation. Individual items (steaks, chops, fish) can be deceptively complicated with larger groups. If you serve meat, everyone has his or her own preference for how it should be cooked. Fish requires careful attention because it cooks quickly. Trying to prepare eight perfectly grilled tuna steaks without ignoring your guests can be tricky.

Nature of the Occasion • Holidays like Thanksgiving and Christmas call for specific foods; anniversary parties or birthday celebrations require more festive menus than a quiet dinner for four friends. Remember that large budgets do not necessarily translate into fabulous food. I have found that a treasured family recipe can lend a greater sense of occasion to a menu than an expensive cut of meat. If you have a reputation for making "the best" deviled eggs, spaghetti sauce or carrot cake and you prepare the celebrated dish, your guests will feel privileged that you have honored them with your efforts.

Guests' Enthusiasm for Food • I have learned from experience those of my guests who quiver upon seeing a homemade chocolate soufflé and those who are satisfied with a dish of ice cream. Don't spend countless hours in the kitchen preparing a complicated recipe if you know your dinner guests are not food enthusiasts. I have two very dear friends whom I love to entertain but I've learned that four fork-fulls of "take-out Chinese" elicits the same response as my recipe for coq au vin. Unless I'm in the mood to cook and have a surplus of free time, I choose the simpler option.

Going It Alone • Menu planning is always affected by the number of people assisting you in the kitchen. Whether it's a spouse, loved one, relative, friend or hired help, an extra pair of "informed hands" allows for more complicated menus. I define "informed hands" as anyone who has a thorough working knowledge of your kitchen and will do exactly as they are told. Never accept assistance from well-meaning individuals who may not know where the serving spoons, bottle openers, dish towels and pepper are kept. They'll plague you with unnecessary questions which will frustrate your efforts. Helpers who insist upon offering (and implementing) their suggestions on everything from the best salad-tossing method to the correct size for a slice of cake can be equally irritating. If you know you will be entertaining on your own, make menu choices that do not require a great deal of last-minute preparation.

Experimentation • Experimenting with new recipes and ideas is what keeps your entertaining style alive. Most hosts who love to cook will browse through magazines or the food sections of newspapers looking for new and exciting ways of preparing tried and true foods. If you find a recipe you've never prepared, experiment on a group of close friends or relatives—just in case the result is not quite what you had anticipated. Several years ago I attended a Christmas dinner in Dallas. In honor of my visit the energetic hostess had decided to prepare stuffed cornish hens—something she had *never* done before. Her presentation was beautiful but when the guests cut into the Christmas birds they were somewhat agitated by the sight of "raw hen." The horrified hostess had to clear the table and try again. It took her two more attempts until the hens were thoroughly cooked; by then, the guests (myself included) had lost their appetites.

Business Entertaining • The purpose of business entertaining is to allow you to get to know your business acquaintances more intimately and discuss specific business ventures or proposals. If you choose complicated, time-consuming menus that require your presence in the kitchen you will be defeating the purpose of the event. Whenever I organize a business luncheon in my home I select menus that can be prepared *entirely* in advance. Cold items are the easiest. Poached salmon or grilled chicken accompanied by a vegetable salad on a bed of lettuce can be assembled on individual plates and stored in the refrigerator. After you seat your guests all you have to do is remove the plates from your refrigerator and serve. For desserts choose simple items such as pies and cakes (which can be sliced and arranged on plates ahead of time) or individual cups of mousse or custard (again, prepared ahead of time and placed in the refrigerator). An efficiently organized and executed business luncheon or dinner will inspire confidence in your professional abilities.

Planning a menu should be fun. If you find yourself making choices which you dread preparing or dislike eating, choose again. If you don't approach the menu-planning process with an enthusiastic spirit, it can't help but affect the outcome. There is no better testament to the transformational powers of a carefully selected menu than the film, *Babette's Feast*, which so delightfully depicts a group of bickering friends who find harmony through a magnificently planned and prepared five-course meal.

Music

One of the main objectives of entertaining is to provide your guests with a few hours of escape from a world full of work and worry. A truly successful dinner party unfolds like a delightful one-act play: the characters (guests) reveal information about who they are and what they want; after a drink or

> "And the night shall be filled with music,
> And the cares that infest the day,
> Shall fold their tents like the Arabs,
> And silently steal away."
>
> —Henry Wadsworth Longfellow

two, the action beings to stir; there are a few lively confrontations and colorful stories; (hopefully) by the end of the evening everyone has been united in at least one meaningful moment which irrevocably alters the relationships in a positive way. The importance of music in orchestrating these events cannot be underestimated.

◆ Musical considerations

Plan Ahead • As with all other aspects of entertaining do as much as you can ahead of time. Don't wait until your guests have arrived and then stand in front of the stereo, pawing through your CDs and cassettes trying to decide what to play. A few hours before my guests are scheduled to arrive

I select an assortment of at least five different CDs to alternate throughout the evening. I believe that stereos should be heard and not seen. If you choose the music before your guests arrive you can alternate selections throughout the evening without drawing a great deal of attention to what you are doing. And if you own a five-disc rotating CD carousel, so much the better.

Type of Function • Make musical selections based on the purpose of the gathering. It is a family get-together? A business luncheon or dinner? A party for friends? For business-related entertaining I prefer subdued instrumentals (classical or jazz) because they don't compete with the conversation. When entertaining friends, I mix an assortment of popular and dance music, often making my own mix of songs for a particular occasion.

Guest List • Examine your guest list and make musical choices that will stimulate everyone. Whenever possible, research individual preferences. You'll make a definite impression during a romantic dinner if you pop open a bottle of champagne while playing your special guest's favorite song.

Consider Conversation • Unless you're throwing a wild dance party, music should not be played at a volume that makes it impossible to have a conversation. Sound levels should be influenced by both the purpose of the function and the guest list.

Pacing • Musical pacing applies to both volume and style. I usually begin the evening slowly with soft music so that the first guests to arrive don't feel as if they're walking into an empty club. As more guests arrive and the room fills with the sounds of laughter and conversation, gradually increase the volume and alternate your musical selections to increasingly upbeat songs. I often change the music when the guests sit down to dinner because it helps to establish a transition.

Gauge the Reaction of Your Guests • Do not ignore the reaction of your guests to the type of music you are playing. If you make a selection and it doesn't seem to be enhancing the mood don't hesitate to change the music.

Be Accommodating Whenever Possible • Certain guests may make musical requests; some may even be so bold as to browse through your collection and change the music themselves. Try to handle these situations as diplomatically as possible. Ask the individual what type of music he or she prefers. Try and honor the request if you feel it won't interfere with the mood of the party. But if someone is adamant about playing *Beethoven's Fifth* or *West Side Story* during a quiet dinner for six don't feel shy about saying "no." Make an excuse: "I listened to that all afternoon," "it skips," or "the tape is broken."

Live Music • Live musicians make a wonderful addition for large parties and outdoor entertaining but I find them out of place for very small functions. I once attended a dinner party for four where we were serenaded by a trio consisting of harp, cello and violin. Although the music was lovely I felt uncomfortable making conversation during dinner with the musicians less than three feet away. Live music works best in large spaces for large groups.

No Music? • I once entertained a playwright who had not been in my apartment for more than ten minutes before he asked if I would turn the music off: he wanted to engage in a stimulating conversation and be able to concentrate on the voices in the room. I happily obliged; no one has ever made a better case for the absence of music during conversation.

Carefully chosen music is like a special ingredient in a recipe: it intensifies a flavor already present and creates a pleasantly lingering image in one's memory.

Outlines & Lists

Organization is one of the keys to successful entertaining. The process of orchestrating an ensemble of food, friends, flowers and forks to produce one enchanted evening requires careful planning. There are hundreds of decisions to be made from the moment you decide to extend an invitation until the last guest departs. The more events you organize, the less you'll need lists; party planning will eventually become as routine as getting dressed.

◆ The week before the event

The following tasks can be performed as soon as you decide to organize a party but should be completed no later than one week before the scheduled event to avoid last-minute rushing about.

Select a Menu • One of the most time-consuming elements of entertaining is food preparation. The menu may affect many of the other decisions you have to make regarding table settings, flowers or alcohol. Selecting a menu as early as possible will allow you to enjoy the process of shopping, organizing, and preparing for your party. (See "Menu Planning.")

Create a Master Shopping List of Everything You Need to Purchase • To avoid making repeated trips to numerous stores, create a master shopping list that contains everything you need. Review each of the selected recipes, carefully writing down the ingredients you need to purchase. Don't forget to add such necessary items as paper towels, candles, non-alcoholic beverages, cleaning supplies (if you're using silver make sure you have silver polish on the list), bathroom tissues and towels, cooking and serving utensils, pots, pans, and platters. Use the master shopping list to make a "store-by-store" shopping list, deciding which items can be purchased from which particular stores. Keep a separate list for each shop you visit, crossing off the supplies as they are purchased. There is nothing worse than realizing a half hour before dinner that you forgot the dressing for the salad or the lemon for the hollandaise sauce.

Purchase Non-perishable Items • Using your "store-by-store" shopping list, buy everything that won't spoil in a week's time. I usually do my big shop at this time, excluding such items as fish, meat and certain fruits and vegetables.

Purchase the Necessary Alcohol • Based upon your budget, menu, and the type of event, select and purchase all of the required alcohol. Early shopping will allow you ample time to compare prices and visit discount stores.

Choose the Table Setting • Select the china, crystal and silver. Make sure you have enough pieces for the table setting; examine each piece for chips and cracks.

◆ The day before the event

The day before the event is the busiest period in the entertainment schedule—often more hectic than the party itself. Doing as much as possible ahead of time will maximize your ability to relax before, during and after the party.

Buy All Perishable Items • The following items should be bought 1–2 days before the party: fish, meat, certain fruits and vegetables, and flowers.

Set the Table • Setting a beautiful table takes time and should not be done in a rushed manner. If you're using your prized family silver, clean each piece (I use the liquid dip) a few hours before setting the table (see "Setting the Table").

Clean Your Home • The cleanliness of your home will affect your guests' ability to relax. Pay special attention to the guest bathroom, making sure it's stocked with the necessary supplies (see "Bathrooms").

Chill Wine, Beer, Champagne and All Necessary Beverages • I always prefer beverages (both alcoholic and non-alcoholic) which have been chilled overnight. Make sure you don't bury the bottles in the back of a refrigerator. Place them in a visible and easily accessible location.

Check Your Ice Supply • Don't ever run out!

Organize the Front Closet • If you use your front hall closet for storage, clear the space the day (or days) before the party to make room for coats. Don't forget to check the supply of hangers.

Confirm the Guest List • I always telephone my guests the day before to (a) remind them of the time and place of the party, and (b) tell them how much I look forward to their company. Confirming the guest list reduces the possibility of "no-shows."

Select all the Serving Platters and Utensils You Will Need • Based upon the menu and style of service (individual plates or "family style"), choose all of the necessary items; examine them for chips and cracks before washing.

◆ The day of the event

Check the Table Setting • I always examine the table setting a few hours before the party is scheduled to begin; if necessary, I make last-minute adjustments, adding or removing place settings based upon the confirmation list. If you're using placecards, decide upon the seating arrangements.

Organize the Flowers and Centerpiece • If you're acting as the florist for the occasion, create the flower arrangements and centerpieces after your home is clean and the table has been set.

Light the Scented Candles Two Hours Before Your Party Is Scheduled to Begin • (See "Candles & Incense.")

Select and Organize the Music Before the Guests Arrive • (See "Music.")

Prepare the Coffee and Tea Trolley • (See "Coffee & Tea.")

Sequence of Dinner • A few hours before the party, make a list of what you need to remember to make the dinner run smoothly; if necessary, use yellow post-its on the stove, refrigerator, or individual plates to remind you what to do. As you perform the task, remove the post-it and toss it in the garbage. Such reminders may include: oven timing sequence ("bake potatoes at 400 degrees"; "remove potatoes, reduce heat to 'warm' and place pie in oven"); "pour salad dressing" (I have a tendency to forget this so I still use a sticker to remind myself); "ice cream in freezer for pie." I have, on occasion, become so involved in the conversation that I forget the salad course or the gravy bowl. Keep a list on the refrigerator of everything on the menu and review it before sitting down to dinner.

Remember that outlines and lists are meant to help you organize an event so you can relax. Don't become obsessed to the point where you spend half the evening reviewing a collection of yellow post-its attached to every surface in the kitchen. As a general rule, if the outlines and lists increase your panic level (because you feel overwhelmed by what they require you to do) you have too many; if the notes increase your confidence and sense of control, you have just enough.

Pets

Entertaining in the presence of animals can turn an elegant affair into a scatterbrained segment from David Letterman's "Stupid Pet Tricks." Although a beloved pet has the ability to transform a furnished space into a loving home it is not necessarily the life of every party. We have all witnessed the over-affectionate dog who develops an unnatural attraction to a guest's leg or the defiant feline who insists on scrutinizing the table setting when the guests are seated. As a proud pet owner and responsible host, it is important to decide whether you are going to limit the interaction between pet and guest. The decision should be based on (a) the size and style of the event, and (b) what is in the best interests of both your pet and the guests.

◆ Pet proposals

Size of event • The larger the party the less desirable it is to allow your pet to roam freely. Unless your dog finds the presence of strangers relaxing, confine the animal to a private area of your home. I find large groups make most animals nervous; it is also difficult to monitor the interaction between the pet and the guests. Some people think that offering a dog a cheese stick or deviled egg is harmless but if eighteen guests have the same idea you may end up with one queasy canine. Small dogs can get trampled in large groups; large dogs crowd a packed space.

Style of Event • For formal or business entertaining, the presence of cats, dogs or other pets can be distracting. Ardent animal lovers excluded, guests in black tie and expensive evening wear are not often receptive to overly affectionate animals. I once worked for an eccentric heiress who overcame what she felt was the stumbling block between formal functions and her "babies": she hired an internationally famous designer to create tuxedos and magnificent evening gowns for each of her ten toy poodles. The "doggiewear" (as the guests referred to it) was certainly the talk of the party.

Allergies • If you are inviting someone into your home for the first time, you may want to mention that you own a pet to which the guest may be allergic. Certain people have very strong reactions to cat hair. If you are aware of this, place the cat in a separate room and vacuum thoroughly an hour before the guest arrives. If a guest informs you about his (or her) allergies after arriving, apologize and place your pet in another room.

Fears • Never embarrass or try to conquer the fears of a guest who is frightened by the presence of a particular animal. Whether it's a playful puppy or a slithering snake, respect the person's feelings and remove the "frightening" creature. Remember that not everyone reacts to animals in the same way. I once interviewed for a job with an extremely charming but eccentric Englishwoman who adored furry creatures. While I was seated upon a green leather sofa in her drawing room I felt something tickling my neck. Imagine my surprise when I looked down and saw a rat nibbling my earlobe. Without so much as batting a well-mascarraed eyelash, my prospective employer introduced me to "Horace" and continued with the interview. While I found Horace delightful, others did not. Several months after I had accepted the position I was serving a very formal tea to a room full of society matrons. Horace (who had an affinity for fur) decided to take a nap on Lady Hermione's sable-collared jacket. As soon as the dignified matron saw what she termed "a vile and filthy rodent attaching itself to my personage," she began to run around the drawing room as if she were on fire. My employer explained he was harmless but the matron quickly departed.

No Begging Allowed! • If you allow pets to roam freely during a particular function make sure they don't continually harass the guests by requesting an endless supply of food or affection. It is annoying and embarrassing for guests if your dog is constantly jumping into their laps, begging for biscuits, or using their shoes as a chewing bone. If the pet is not trained or disciplined it should be kept in a separate room. It is not fair to the animal to expect it to suddenly adopt a new set of rules and regulations just because you have guests. And it is not fair to your guests to be subjected to an uncontrollable pet. My cocker spaniel has been trained in canine etiquette for all occasions: she never jumps into a lap unless invited; she never begs for or takes food from a plate unless it is offered. She might peer longingly from the corner of a room as you devour a steaming lamb chop but she would never be so bold as to approach you directly, demanding her fair share.

Noise • If you have a bird, cat or dog who chatters endlessly realize that although you may find it charming and be used to the sounds, your guests may find it unnerving.

When deciding what to do with your pet during a particular function, try and realize that not all of your friends may regard your precious pit bull or capricious cat as the child you never had. Remember: "Man's best friend can be a guest's worst nightmare."

Placecards

Placecards serve two important functions when entertaining:

> **1.** They allow the host or hostess to control the seating arrangement; and
> **2.** They help to enhance the mood for a particular occasion.

The arrangement of guests at the dinner table is equally as important as the combination of ingredients for a treasured family recipe: one incorrect item carelessly tossed into the pot and the flavor is irrevocably altered. As with flowers, there is a fine art in "people arranging," taking into account an individual's interests, profession and *marital status*:

I am not an advocate, however, of abandoning unmarried or unpartnered guests to a particular area or table. It only makes them feel as if they are suffering from some dreaded social disease.

> To ensure harmony, single women, divorcees, and females who have recently appeared on magazine covers *must* never be seated next to the husbands of jealous wives.

Physical details such as height, weight, and whether someone is right-or left-handed also help inform the host. I once attended a dinner party and was seated across from two large-framed guests: one left-handed; the other right-handed. It was a true test of will to suppress my laughter during the first course: As the sizable couple attempted to eat their respective salads, elbows began colliding, propelling thinly sliced cucumbers into the air. By the time the chocolate soufflé had been served the frustrated couple had worked out an (unspoken) agreement: Using their peripheral vision as discreetly as possible, they took turns raising their knives, forks and spoons. A carefully arranged set of placecards could have prevented the uncomfortable situation.

Placecards can also be used to create a sense of fun or enhance a particular mood. From a romantic dinner for two to a birthday party for fifteen extremely energetic five-year-olds, placecards help to make any event special.

Placecard holders are the first requirement. These range in price and style and can include everything from pieces of Styrofoam and inexpensive trinkets sold at card stores to silver and gold-plated objects from Tiffany's. The most traditional and formal use of placecards is to inscribe each guest's name (in black ink) on a small white card. Each card is then inserted into a silverplated holder. For formal occasions, titles such as Mrs., Mr., Miss, Ms., Dr., Lord, Countess, etc. should be used before each name. Women used to be identified by their husband's name (i.e., Jane Taylor, wife of John Taylor, would have a placecard which read "Mrs. *John* Taylor"—not "Mrs. *Jane* Taylor"). Very few people—especially in America—maintain this type of formality anymore.

A particularly affluent household I once managed hired a professional calligrapher to inscribe over 500 names (friends, relatives, and business associates) on elegant placecards edged in 24-carat gold. For each party I would retrieve the necessary cards (alphabetically arranged, of course) from an ivory box which was stored in the drawer of a Louis XV cabinet. After I placed each card in a fourteen-carat gold rectangular holder the mistress of the house would sit in each chair and imagine herself engaged in conversation with the person on her left and right. She was rather eccentric and extremely formal; she felt that only by sitting in each chair and gaining the perspective of each guest could she truly perfect her seating arrangement.

I prefer a more informal approach to entertaining, using specially chosen postcards as placecards. This approach is both fun and inexpensive. When entertaining individuals in the publishing or entertainment industries I use Annie Leibovitz photocards or pictures of Hollywood stars. I print each guest's name (in black pen) on small white labels placed at the top (or bottom) of each card.

You can choose postcards to suit an occasion. To help evoke the appropriate ambiance for a romantic dinner, you might select a postcard of an impressionist painting or a seductive photograph with the nickname of your loved one inscribed at the top. For a children's party I once organized we used postcards of Disney characters which were inserted into apples. At the end of the party we gave the colorful cartoon characters (and apples) as party-favors.

Photographs are a fun substitute for postcards. If you have a new picture of your three year old that you wish to present to your relatives, why not invite them to dinner, using the photograph as a placecard. You can print "Grand-mother" or "Aunt Mary" on removable labels attached to the bottom of each photo. It's a fun way to receive a photo-graph—especially at family birthday parties.

I always give the placecards to guests when they leave. If someone forgets his or her "souvenir," I write a brief note on the back and mail it. Like photographs, the cards serve as a remembrance of the particular occasion. My mother (at last count) has collected 143 cards over the past twenty-five years, carefully arranged in a silk-covered photograph album. Twice a year she reviews the collection, recounting specific parties and celebrations. Used in this manner, place-cards can become small sign posts in one's life, marking the memorable events along the way.

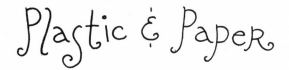

Plastic & Paper

Under the appropriate circumstances, entertaining with plastic and paper products can be:

1. *Time-saving*

2. *Practical*

3. *Cost-effective*

4. *Creative*

Only a snob would negate the possibilities of plastic and paper products. There are certain occasions when fine china, silver and crystal are not only *impractical* but *inappropriate*. Last summer I was invited by a Southampton socialite to an outdoor luncheon. Two round tables of eight had been beautifully set with an assortment of Wedgewood, Bacarrat and Christofle. It was a brilliantly sunny day; while the ocean breezes worked wonders at cooling off the crowd, they did little to alleviate the temperature of the sun-lit silver. It was quite amusing when the group sat down to lunch: some guests cried out in shock as they attempted to lift knives, forks and spoons which felt as if they were on fire; others used the white linen napkins as protective gloves, wrapping them around the scorching silver. The host was embarrassed to say the least. She could have saved herself the humiliation by either covering the tables with a canopy (I never advise setting tables in direct sunlight) or overcoming her attitude about what she once referred to as "the commoner's cutlery."

If you still doubt that paper and plastic products have their own special niche within the entertaining world, read on.

◆ Time- and money-saving benefits

No Silver to Be Polished • Most people cannot afford the luxury of a houseman, butler or maid who will transform forty-eight pieces of tarnished metal into a collection of sparkling silver. For an average dinner for eight, it would take at least an hour of hand polishing. With plastic products all you have to do is rip open a bag and you're ready to set the table.

Clearing the Table Is Simplified • Instead of carefully balancing plates and making several trips from the table to the kitchen, plastic and paper plates can be stacked on top of each other; the table can be cleared at one time— and most of what's cleared gets thrown away, not washed. The less time you have to spend in the kitchen, the more time you can spend with your guests.

No Laundry or Ironing of Linens • Only those of you who entertain with cloth napkins and tablecloths on a regular basis know the "joy" of pressing eight Irish linen placemats with matching dinner and desert napkins, not to mention large tablecloths. If I decide to use matching linen for a dinner party for eight, the dry cleaning bill usually exceeds $50 (this includes placemats or a table cloth with matching cocktail, dinner and desert napkins). The cleaning cost exceeds the most extravagant estimate for purchasing paper and plastic products. And if I use the linen I still have to wash the dishes and silver myself.

◆ **Practicality**

Increased Safety for Outdoor Entertaining • I usually recommend using plastic and paper products for outdoor entertaining—certainly for any events which are located near a pool. Broken glass or china is an outdoor hazard. No matter how carefully you clean shattered glass, it's impossible to be sure you haven't missed a sliver.

Increased Safety When Entertaining Children • For family affairs and children's parties I recommend using products which, if broken, will not create a safety hazard. Children have an easier time manipulating plastic knives and cups because they are lightweight.

◆ **Creative Applications**

Special Occasions • Card stores carry a festive assortment of matching paper products suitable for bridal and baby showers, engagement parties, birthdays, and holidays. Pick a color or design element in the paper products and incorporate it into your table settings and centerpiece.

Children's Parties • Most children would rather eat from a plate bearing the face of a familiar cartoon character than the finest Limoges. I once organized a children's party using an enormous sheet of white paper for a tablecloth. Each child's place setting featured a white Styrofoam cup (turned upside down) with an assortment of Crayola crayons arranged like flowers. During the party the children created a tablecloth far more colorful and imaginative than anything I could have bought.

Mix and Match Colors • Because plastic and paper products come in such a wonderful array of colors, I love to mix and match colors for particular events. For a Fourth of July picnic I created a festive pattern on the buffet table with red, white and blue plates, napkins, forks, spoons, and knives. I once set a table for a sit-down luncheon for eight using a different color for each place setting—a spectacular sight—though not the most cost effective.

◆ **Plastic and paper pointers**

   1. The best occasions to use paper products are: large parties; children's parties; summer/outdoor entertaining; buffets; holidays; lunches and brunches.
   2. Paper products are not suitable for: sit-down dinners; business dinners; groups of four or less.
   3. The use of paper products will affect the menu. Don't serve dishes that contain liquids (stews, casseroles, anything with sauce). A soggy paper plate can prove quite challenging when you're trying to clear the table.
   4. When using paper products outdoors be sure to

tape or weight down the tablecloth and napkins. This will save you the embarrassment of running into your neighbor's yard to retrieve half the table setting.

5. Be environmentally aware of how many paper and plastic products you use. Whenever possible, purchase products that have been made from recycled goods.

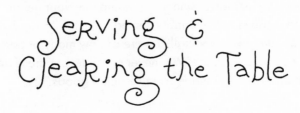

Serving & Clearing the Table

A host is like a professional juggler: coupling a talent for precision timing with an ability to smile under the most stressful circumstances, the host manipulates a multitude of elements for the sole purpose of entertaining and amusing the crowd. Every host—like every juggler—strives for the appearance of effortless entertaining. No matter how many hours you may have invested in preparing for a dinner party, that time will have been for naught if you are anxious, agitated, and resultantly accident-prone when serving the meal and clearing the table.

Unless you entertain frequently, you may not appreciate a host's ability to serve a three-course dinner for eight guests without appearing flustered. We've all sat at dinner tables where it became painfully apparent that the host extended too many invitations or made impractical menu choices: a five-minute lapse between the time the first two guests and the rest of the table is served; presenting the dessert before the dinner plates have been cleared; dirty dishes strewn across every kitchen surface; an absentee host.

You don't have to hire extra help to ensure "smooth serving." You must, however, develop a method for executing the task with a minimal amount of fuss and frustration. The following suggestions will help organize your efforts.

◆ Serving and clearing considerations

Don't Carry More Than You Can Handle • Unless you've worked as a professional waiter and have mastered the skill of balancing six steaming dinner plates across two perfectly balanced arms—don't try it! Most people cannot manage more than two plates (one in each hand) at a time.

Serve and Clear in an Orderly Fashion • I always serve the ladies first, starting with the first female guest to right of the host's place setting, working clockwise around the table. After all of the ladies have been served I begin with the first gentleman to the right of the host, working again in a clockwise direction.

Always serve from the right and clear from the left. When guests are finished with a specific course they should place their knives, forks, and spoons in a vertical position in the center of the plate: the fork prongs and the spoon bowl facing upward; the curve of the knife pointing toward the plate. If your guests fail to position their cutlery in the correct position (and many will) do not draw attention to the minor faux pas by laughing hysterically and labeling them "cultural clods" or "social simpletons." Make a silent adjustment before clearing to lessen the likelihood of flying forks and soaring spoons as you begin to lift the plates from the table. Remember to clear the entire table before serving the next course.

Off of the Table and into the Dishwasher • Many hosts make the mistake of adding an extra step between clearing the table and loading the dishwasher by stacking dirty dishes on kitchen counters. It takes less than ten seconds to empty, rinse and stack a plate in the dishwasher—assuming, of course, that your dishwasher is empty (see "Cleaning Up") and your kitchen is properly organized (see "Kitchens"). Used cutlery can either be placed in the dishwasher or in a small tub filled with soapy water. By immediately loading plates into the dishwasher you (a) simplify the cleaning process once your guests have departed, (b) reduce the possibility of lingering food odors, (c) keep counters free for working your way through the rest of the meal, and (d) maintain a clean, ordered kitchen which should bolster your self-confidence.

Clearing the Main Course • After your guests have finished the main course, the table must be properly cleared before serving dessert. Remove the charger (or liner) plates at the same time you clear the dinner plate by lifting them as one unit. In addition, the following items should be removed at this time: empty or unused wine glasses; salt and pepper shakers; napkin rings; extra pieces of cutlery from earlier courses which were never used; placecards (optional: I leave them on but many hosts prefer to remove them). The only items remaining should be: the dessert fork and spoon (or knife, as necessary); water glass; champagne glass (if you are serving champagne with dessert); placecard (if you so choose). If one of your guests has used bread crumbs, lettuce leaves or peas to transform their place setting into an abstract design you may want to quietly wipe the table before continuing with the next course. I normally allow my guests to rest for 15–30 minutes (based upon how well the conversation is flowing) before serving dessert.

Clearing the Dessert Course • If, following the dessert course, my guests prefer moving back to the living room for coffee, tea, liqueurs, and chocolates, I don't clear the dessert dishes. Once the group has relocated, I dim the lights over the dining room. If, however, the conversation is flowing and the guests would prefer to remain at the table, I clear the dessert plates and the accompanying silver.

Using Trolleys • Collapsible trolleys that can easily be stored in a closet are preferable. By stacking the plates on the trolley and then wheeling it to table-side I can serve (and clear) all of the plates in one trip. I first experimented with these "waiters on wheels" during a luncheon for a few friends. I double-stacked the dessert plates, which featured an assortment of berries with a spoon of fresh cream. While I was wheeling the trolley table-side I ran over my cocker spaniel's favorite toy—a small white Gund teddybear. My accident jolted the plates and a multi-colored selection of berries into the air and onto the floor. Unless you're trying to amuse your guests with the sight of flying food, don't stack plates on a trolley.

Remember that the key to serving and clearing a table is making it appear effortless. Any host who takes the time and trouble can become a master in plate-presentation. As my second grade teacher used to say, "Practice and patience are prerequisites for proficiency."

Setting the Table

Anyone traumatized by the prospect of organizing an assortment of forks, knives, spoons, plates and glasses into a perfectly set table for eight merely lacks the information necessary to relax and enjoy the process. Questions regarding table settings are definitely in the top-five list of "What Do You Ask a Professional Majordomo."

- *"Do you set the silver according to the size or the order in which it is used?"*

- *"What are charger plates and do I need to use them for every dinner party?"*

- *"Is it really necessary to set more than one knife, fork and spoon?"*

- *"Are the knives supposed to face toward or away from the plate?"*

- *"Does anyone really care if the knives face toward or away from the plate?"*

The following is a recommendation of how *I* prefer to set a table. It is not meant to be "the definitive method" but merely reflects my own opinions based upon my experiences. As with all aspects of entertaining, adapt suggestions and make choices that suit your own entertaining style.

salt
pepper
placecard
wine glass (white)
water glass
wine glass (red)
champagne glass

Bread/butter plate
Napkin
Bread/butter knife
Salad fork
Dinner fork
Dessert fork
Charger or Dinner plate
Dessert spoon
Dinner knife
Salad knife
Soup spoon

◆ Set the table the day before

Whether you're organizing a buffet or a sit-down dinner, always set the table the day before the event. I allot myself at least an hour when I feel reasonably certain I won't be interrupted: it's very easy to forget a fork or knife if you're constantly distracted. Just as a painter should not rush through the process of applying color to canvas, neither should a host hurry when constructing an esthetically pleasing table setting. Completing the work the day before allows distance from your efforts; you can examine the setting on the day of the event with a "well-rested" but scrutinizing eye.

◆ Organizing the place setting

Plates • The place setting will vary somewhat based upon the particular menu. For a typical four-course meal (soup, salad, main course and dessert) you will need the following six types of plates: charger (sometimes called a liner), bread and butter, soup bowl, salad, dinner, and dessert. A charger plate goes in the center of each place setting, with the bread and butter plate at its far left. The remaining four plates (soup, salad, main course and dessert) should be stacked in the kitchen according to size where they will be used as each course is presented. Leave room for the silver. If you need extra room at the table you can position the bread and butter dish to the *upper* left of the charger plate. In very formal households the charger plate is removed following the soup course, but I prefer to keep it on the table until after the main course. It not only provides a frame for each plate but it also protects the table surface from very hot dishes.

Forks, Knives and Spoons • Separate dining utensils for each course prevent the taste of different foods from mixing together: you wouldn't want the salad dressing on the fork from the salad course influencing the taste of the poached salmon during the main course. I prefer to set the silver in the order in which it is to be used, working from the outside in. For a typical four-course meal the arrangement from left to right would be as follows: bread and butter knife (resting on the right side of the bread and butter plate); salad fork; dinner fork; dessert fork; (the charger plate in the middle); dessert spoon; dinner knife; salad knife; soup spoon.

Some hosts prefer to arrange the cutlery by size with the largest pieces framing the plate. The problem with this arrangement is that your guests must have a working knowledge of the various pieces. Some people might not be able to recognize the difference between a fish fork, dinner fork and salad fork. Why place a guest in an unnecessarily uncomfortable position?

The most popular variation for table settings is to place the dessert fork and spoon above the plate. I find this choice claustrophobic: to me, framing the charger plate with silver on three sides detracts from the overall setting and crowds the area above the plate.

Glasses • For most dinner parties I use three glasses—water, wine and champagne—positioned in a grouping above the silver on the right side of the plate. If you are serving both a fish and meat course accompanied by the customary white and red wines, you must set two wine glasses at each place setting.

Placecards • Placecards should be positioned directly above the center of the charger plate.

Salt and Pepper • I prefer using silver-plated miniature salt and pepper cellars, placed to the left of the placecards. If you have the money to invest ($50–$100 a pair), Cartier and Christofle offer a wonderful selection which will certainly delight your guests.

◆ Tablecloths, placemats and napkins

Deciding whether to use a tablecloth or placemats is based upon (a) the design concept of your dining area, and (b) the formality of the occasion. I have an unusual dining table, and I like to arrange the place settings directly on the table surface.

Colorful and decorative placemats are perfect for breakfasts, brunches and luncheons. Fine lace, damask, and embroidered linen tablecloths—which require careful maintenance—are usually reserved for very special occasions. Combining two different tablecloths can add color and contrast to an otherwise simple table setting. Try mixing round over rectangular shapes, and prints over solids.

Napkins can be folded and arranged in a variety of shapes, with or without napkin rings, placed in either the center of the plate, resting on the bread and butter dish or underneath the silver framing the right side of the place setting.

Approach setting the table with a sense of fun and adventure, and you'll find it can be an amazingly entertaining experience.

Smoking

Deciding whether to allow guests to smoke in your home is a personal decision. As a non-smoker living in a completely white apartment, I prefer that my guests refrain from smoking at all times. Through the years I have experimented with the following approaches for confronting this sensitive issue without offending anyone.

◆ Ways to discourage smoking

Place a Sign on Your Front Door • By placing a small sign on your front door that discourages smoking you are able to address the issue from the moment the guest arrives. The sign allows you to communicate this message without a direct confrontation. The front door of my apartment displays a 4-inch square sign with black on white print that reads, KINDLY RESPECT MY HOME: REMOVE YOUR SHOES AND REFRAIN FROM SMOKING. Signs like this should be at eye level, and easy to read. They are not meant to be a design statement, color coordinated with your apartment or elaborately printed. Most guests will be gracious about respecting your policy when it is addressed in this manner, either refraining from smoking while they are in your home or excusing themselves to smoke a cigarette in the hallway or outdoors.

Remove All Ashtrays, Lighters and Matches •
One of the best ways to enforce a "no smoking" policy is to
refrain from decorating your home with objects that encourage smoking. Even if you own a beautiful Lalique ashtray or
a priceless antique Cartier table lighter don't display objects
associated with smoking. Your actions will create a mixed
message which may encourage someone to smoke. If there
are no ash trays, lighters or matches in sight a smoker (despite having read your sign) will be forced to ask you for
assistance. Addressing the subject before a cigarette is actually lit is less awkward.

"Smoke-free" Ashtrays • Certain companies
have developed "smoke-free" ashtrays: containers with
built-in fans that supposedly draw the smoke from a burning
cigarette into the base of the mechanism. I personally do not
advocate the use of these devices. Even if they support their
claim they don't purify the air of the carcinogens that a
smoker exhales with each puff. Nor do they address the issue
of sloppy smokers who allow ashes to fall onto the carpet
and floors or burn holes in the furniture.

Substitutions and Distractions • Certain people
use cigarettes in social situations as props or to satisfy oral
cravings. Offer them a drink or an hors d'oeuvre as a substitute. Involve them in a lively conversation or ask them to assist
you in the kitchen—anything active that might take their mind
off smoking.

Reasonable Answers • If one of your guests con-
fronts you directly—asking why you prohibit smoking in your
home—answer with one of the following responses:

162

• *Explain that in the past you have had to repair and replace furniture and carpeting because of accidents related to smoking.*

• *If you are in the presence of children or pregnant women even the most addicted smokers will not push the issue. I once told an aggressive smoker who loved animals that Lulu, my miniature cocker spaniel, was pregnant; she immediately withdrew her request and congratulated me.*

• *Tell the guest that you are asthmatic; the presence of any type of smoke induces coughing fits.*

• *Politely explain your concerns about the effects of secondary smoke.*

◆ Final suggestions

Don't Preach • Your job is to implement your policy without offending anyone—not to convert smokers into non-smokers.

Always Be Polite • Don't judge people who smoke or treat them as second-class citizens. Answer their smoking requests in a calm, rational manner.

The "Buddy System" • If one of your guests excuses himself to smoke a cigarette in the hallway (or outdoors) try and find a fellow smoker to accompany the individual. If time allows (and you don't mind) escort the smoker yourself. This will allow you time to speak privately with the guest and it won't make the individual feel as if he is being banished to smoker's Siberia.

Avoid Arguments, Debates or Physical Confrontations • If, despite your many requests, someone decides to light a cigarette in your home, do not remove the cigarette from the offending mouth. Rise above the rudeness of the individual for the duration of your party. Telephone the smoker the next day and explain that because he (or she) could not respect your wishes he will no longer be welcome in your home.

If the majority of guests you entertain are gracious and well-mannered you shouldn't experience any difficulties in implementing a "no smoking" policy. In an increasingly health-conscious society it is not as fashionable—or acceptable—as it once was to "light up" after a meal.

Table Gifts

When I worked for an Arab prince I learned the importance of gift-giving to Arabian culture. Whenever we traveled, I often felt like the proprietor of a duty-free shop, carrying an assortment of Cartier watches, expensive lighters, Hermés scarves and assorted jewelry and gems. In the event of a party, each guest had an extravagant memento beautifully wrapped and placed next to his (or her) placecard. Imagine arriving at the dinner table and discovering that instead of the usual soup or smoked salmon your first course consisted of a gold Cartier Santos watch. While most of us are not financially capable of such lavish gift-giving, we can incorporate small tokens into place settings that will make any guest feel special.

Table gifts should be a surprise. If one of your guests were to stroll into the dining room and glance at the table setting, the gifts should look like a decorative part of the overall picture. Only after the guest is seated should it become apparent that the flower in the napkin ring is actually a long stem chocolate rose wrapped in red foil. To help ensure the surprise element make choices that blend in with your table setting and centerpiece.

◆ Common types

Beautifully packaged chocolates are the most commonly used table gifts. They are relatively inexpensive ($1–$3 per place setting) and are available in a wide assortment of shapes and colors. I usually try to buy chocolates that are packaged for a particular occasion or holiday. For Thanksgiving, a small chocolate shaped turkey wrapped in foil adds color and sparkle to an ordinary table setting. Most card shops carry an assortment of inexpensive holiday chocolates. For fall entertaining I prefer to use the four-piece box of chocolates made by Godiva. The rich gold color of the boxes and the silk red rose on top enhance an autumnal place setting. The guests can either eat the chocolates after dinner (you'll find that most don't) or take them home.

Many people offer table gifts at their children's birthday parties but forget to include them when entertaining adults. Colorful tables and unexpected gifts can be just as exciting when you're forty as they were when you were four. Whenever possible, try to choose table gifts that are representative of both you and your guests. One Christmas, I decided to give each of my guests a Tiffany silver-plated bookmark; I incorporated the gift into the table setting. They range between $20–$30 dollars apiece and are available in an assortment of musical instruments, animals, and geometric shapes. As an author who is constantly trying to promote reading I felt these small tokens would express something I believe in; because of the wide assortment, I could choose individual bookmarks with specific people in mind. There is nothing more magical than a Christmas table set with eight miniature blue boxes wrapped in white ribbon. For this particular occasion, I incorporated the Tiffany blue color into the base of the centerpiece: a ceramic bowl which I then planted with white tulips.

◆ Tips on table gifts

1. Table gifts should be small in size so that they do not overpower the table setting. While a four-piece box of chocolates is a lovely gesture, a one-pound box would be inappropriate.

2. When appropriate, table gifts should tie into a specific theme, occasion or holiday.

3. For certain occasions like birthday parties, give gifts with a sense of humor (such as novelty items).

4. Table gifts are perfect for romantic dinners. We've all heard stories of engagement rings hidden in the wine glass or under the dinner plate. Be creatively romantic and surprise your loved one with something special.

5. When your guests leave for the evening remind them to take their gifts.

Telephones & Answering Machines

Modern technology has transformed telephones, answering and facsimile machines into the preferred toys of socially spirited adults. While many households thrive on the frenzied activity of multiple telephones engaged in an electronically produced harmony, your guests may not be enthusiasts of such modern "music." I have attended parties where the telephone literally rang every five minutes. Sometimes a staff member would answer the call and pass along messages to the host; on other occasions the host would pick up on every ring. During one party I attended the host allowed the machine to answer the call but had not adjusted the machine's volume. When the caller began to speak the sound was deafening; the room instantly fell silent. The guests were entertained by a detailed four-minute message from the host's recently divorced wife. She was attributing her ex-husband's inability to pay timely alimony to a certain sexual deviancy coupled with substance abuse. The outburst certainly enlivened an otherwise stuffy occasion. But not in a manner which reflected favorably on the host.

Depending on the frequency

> **"Never let them hear it ring!"**
> —John Teed

with which your telephone rings and the unusual and/or private assortment of messages you receive, the following suggestions will (a) prevent your guests from feeling as if they are in competition for your attention and (b) protect your privacy.

◆ Telephone tips

Before Your Guests Arrive • Turn the volume on your answering machine down and adjust the telephone ringer to "low." This will enable you to screen incoming calls until all of your guests have arrived. Certain guests may telephone to apologize for delays or last-minute cancellations. You need to be able to hear this information without disturbing those guests who have already arrived. If the stereo is playing, position yourself in the room where the telephone is still audible. I once entertained a first-time guest who had lost my address; when she telephoned the stereo was booming at a level which prevented me from hearing the phone ring. I assumed she wasn't coming and was horrified an hour later when I checked my messages and heard her nervously chanting, "Desmond . . . Desmond . . . Are you there? . . . Are you there? . . . Where are you? . . . Where are you? . . ."

After Your Guests Have Arrived • Once all of your guests have arrived, turn the telephone ringers off and the volume on the answering machines down to an inaudible level. I check my answering machine once or twice throughout the evening. If one of my guests informs me that he or she is expecting a call I leave the ringers on. I also make an exception when entertaining the parents of infants whose babysitters may be calling with a question or an update.

Keep All Conversations Brief • If, for any reason, you do answer the telephone while entertaining, keep it short. Inform the caller that you have guests and will call back as soon as possible. If you begin a conversation it is very easy to become involved and distracted. I avoid this potentially awkward situation by never answering the telephone once all of my guests have arrived.

Guests Who Request to Use the Telephone • If one of your guests needs to use the telephone don't ask about the call; allow them to volunteer information, or not. Direct the guest to a private area with a telephone. An office, study, family room or den is more suitable than your kitchen or bedroom. I always assume that if I invite a guest into my home he (or she) is not going to abuse the courtesy, using it as an opportunity to telephone friends in Finland or relatives in Rangoon.

Location of Telephones • Try to have a portable telephone or one with a long extension cord near your main entertaining area. This will enable you to hear the phone; if you need to answer a call you (or one of your guests) can speak in private by walking (or stretching the cord) into another room.

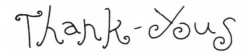

Thank-Yous

I am constantly amazed at the number of guests who *remember* to attend luncheons, dinners, brunches and buffets but *forget* to follow-up with an expression of gratitude. A high-powered agent I spoke with recently stated "it's no longer practical to send a note of thanks—no reasonably minded host expects it. With my calendar, showing up is thanks enough!" She felt that such a burden would take precious minutes out of a schedule that was packed tighter than a New York discoteque on a Saturday night. I strongly disagree, however. *Good manners never go out of fashion.* And although the host may not expect it, if you have the time to drink someone's wine and eat his food, you certainly should take the time to (at the very least) telephone with a brief message of thanks.

◆ **A note of "thanks" serves 3 important functions:**

1. *It acknowledges a guest's appreciation of the host's efforts;*

2. *It assures the host that the guest had a good time; and*

3. *It encourages the host to extend an invitation in the future.*

◆ Time frame

Expressions of gratitude should be communicated as soon after the event as possible—certainly no later than a week. If, for any reason, you realize at some future date that you have forgotten to send a "thank-you" or can't remember, send another, telling your host that you wanted to thank him (or her) again for such a memorable occasion.

◆ Types of "thank-yous"

Cards and Letters • This includes everything from handwritten notes on personally inscribed stationery to traditional "thank-you" cards and post cards. Cards should always be handwritten; while letters may be typed I always prefer (no matter how indecipherable) reading someone's handwritten thanks.

Telephone Calls • If you are pressed for time or feel you want to communicate directly, a telephone call is the most efficient means. Telephoning the host provides you with an opportunity to highlight aspects of the party which you particularly enjoyed. A telephone call is the most personal, if informal, way to say thank-you; it can often be the most meaningful.

Gifts • Appropriate thank-you gifts include the following:

1. plants and flowers
2. a fruit basket
3. a box of chocolates
4. a bottle of wine or champagne

Gifts should be simple and not ostentatious. While a bottle of wine or champagne is a lovely gesture, a case (even if you can afford it) is vulgar. One Manhattan society matron created quite a stir when she began thanking her hosts in an extravagant fashion: she sent $1,000 phalaenopsis orchid plants and so many dozens of roses and French tulips they couldn't all be displayed in one room. As a general rule: if the cost of the "Thank-You" gift exceeds the cost of the party it is considered to be an act of conspicuous consumption.

◆ Unique "thank-yous"

Use your imagination to find a unique way of expressing gratitude, taking into consideration the host's preferences.

1. Find out if the host has a preferred flower, type of wine or champagne.
2. Make your own card using the party invitation or photographs you may have taken. One terribly clever guest sent me a "thank-you" in the form of a newspaper society

column that described my dinner party as the social event of the season.

3. One of the nicest ways to thank someone is to invite them to something else—a dinner, the theatre or a concert.

◆ They're never too young to start

One of the main reasons certain adults are not in the practice of sending "thank-yous" is that they were not taught as children. As soon as a child is old enough to hold a Crayola crayon and transform a blank page into a colorful creation the youngster can be introduced to the concept of sending "thank-you" notes. From my earliest years my mother and grandmother drilled me in the etiquette of expressing one's gratitude. My mother was so organized and efficient that she often had her "thank-you" card purchased, written, stamped and ready to be posted before we had even attended the party. Although this practice is a bit extreme, it is certainly preferable to being negligent in one's appreciation.

The amount of time it takes to thank someone, either verbally or in writing, is a small price to pay for the long-lasting good will it creates.

Unexpected Guests

One of my most vivid childhood memories is sitting with my grandmother on a large flowered sofa watching Eartha Kitt

> **"When entertaining, I've always believed you should throw an extra fish into the pot. You never know when one of your guests might bring a friend."**
>
> **—Eartha Kitt**

perform on British television: she seductively slithered across a series of chaise lounges while singing "Just an Old Fashioned Girl." Thirty years later I saw Miss Kitt perform at a New York cabaret. I was so enchanted by her performance and flooded with memories of my grandmother I sent the sultry songstress an orchid plant and invited her to a luncheon at my apartment. Several days later, to my delight, the quintessential "Catwoman" graciously accepted.

Two hours before her scheduled arrival Miss Kitt telephoned to ask if she could bring a friend to the luncheon. She capped off the request with her "extra fish in the pot" philosophy. Since we had never met and she was venturing into an unfamiliar environment I wanted to be as accommodating as possible to ensure her every comfort; I enthusiastically replied that any friend of hers would certainly be a welcome guest in my home.

The moment I hung up the telephone my heart skipped several English beats. Since this was to be a very special luncheon I had researched Miss Kitt's wining and dining preferences, settling on a menu of Beluga caviar, Dom Perignon champagne, Lobster Thermador and chocolate mousse. Perhaps because of my excitement surrounding the event I had not remembered (as I usually do) to "throw an extra lobster in the pot" or "whip up an extra dessert." (You should always have more than enough food and alcohol on hand to ensure that you are not caught short.) Nor had I purchased an extra chocolate rose wrapped in red foil which would so beautifully enhance each place setting. For two minutes my normally methodical and organized mind burst into a fireworks of confusion. I soon calmed myself, however, utilizing the following steps for overcoming my "Kitt Crisis."

◆ 3 Steps for handling unexpected guests

Assess the Situation

Ask yourself a series of questions pertaining to menu and seating arrangements. If time allows, I recommend writing your options on a piece of paper. Circle the choices you eventually make and then use the list as a plan of attack.

- *If it is a formal sit-down dinner can I comfortably fit another guest at the table? Do I have another complete place setting that matches the table? Should I switch from sit-down to buffet to accommodate the extra guest(s)? Will the additional guest(s), in any way, conflict with anyone else?*

- *Can I stretch the food that I am serving without it*

appearing obvious? This is more easily overcome with buffets or family-styled dinners than a formal sit-down affair. When I was a child, whenever unexpected guests arrived my mother or grand-mother would whisper "FHB" ("Family Hold Back"). Instead of the usual three roasted potatoes we would serve ourselves one or two, making a com-ment about dieting or what a large lunch we had eaten.

• Do I have time to make the necessary adjust-ments?

• Do I feel comfortable about making the changes required to accommodate the extra guests(s)? If you cannot devise a plan without feeling angry, annoyed or tense, it is best to tactfully explain that you cannot entertain the additional guest.

For my Eartha Kitt luncheon I knew it would be simple to set another place setting: I had invited seven guests and my dining banquette can comfortably accommodate eight. Once I passed the seating hurdle I stared at seven perfectly prepared lobster tails. I could either (a) try and locate one lone lobster tail in New York in eighty-three minutes or less, (b) use menu substitutions and creative explanations, or (c) slice up the tails into some abstract creation, explaining that "the British have a rather Picasso-like approach to preparing shellfish." Although I was slightly nervous, I decided that I would do whatever was necessary to ensure the comfort of my special guest. I had waited for over thirty years to enter-tain Miss Kitt as she had once entertained my grandmother and myself: nothing would deter me.

Decide on a Course of Action

Reviewing my list of options I decided to add the additional place setting to the table. I soon realized it was ridiculous to destroy seven perfect lobster tails and seven perfectly prepared chocolate mousses: a menu substitution was definitely in order. With seventy-five minutes to countdown I decided that I would enlist outside help for the food requirements and make the necessary table adjustments myself.

Implement Your Plan Quickly and Quietly

I telephoned a friend who was attending the luncheon and asked him to rush to Balducci's (my neighborhood New York gourmet market) to purchase some lemon chicken and sorbet. I would explain that I was allergic to shellfish but wished to accommodate the gastronomic preferences of my special guest. My friend would politely decline his chocolate mousse by stating he was on a strict diet; in one swift move I would offer the sorbet and everything would fall into place. Instead of placing a chocolate rose on each place setting I set them only in front of the ladies' placecards. And since I didn't know the name of the individual who was escorting Miss Kitt I typed "Eartha's Guest" on the placecard, hoping the somewhat humorous approach would be received in the spirit in which it was intended. With fifteen minutes to go, all of the changes had been made. Miss Kitt's guest was a most charming gentleman; the luncheon proved to be a stimulating and entertaining afternoon of conversation and cuisine.

Although I consider it a breach of good manners to visit unexpectedly around meal time or arrive at a dinner party with an extra guest (or guests) without first telephoning, I would never turn someone away or make a guest feel uncomfortable. There are always friends who have unexpected out-of-town guests whom they might wish to include in the festivities. In such instances, *telephone your host or hostess as soon as possible and explain the situation.* This allows sufficient time to make whatever adjustments are necessary to the menu and table setting.

Weekend Guests

Entertaining weekend guests can either be an enjoyable experience or a never-to-be-repeated fiasco. With multiple menus to plan, and bedrooms and bathrooms to prepare, a weekend in the country requires careful organization. There is nothing worse than surviving two hours of bumper-to-bumper traffic only to be shown into a musty guestroom featuring piles of dirty laundry and stacks of yellowed newspapers clogging every corner. I once accepted a weekend invitation from a journalist who escorted me to a room so jammed full of newspapers, magazines, books and encyclopedias I felt like I was checking into a library. There is little point in inviting friends for the weekend if you are not prepared to extend every possible courtesy to your "extended guests."

The following lists and suggestions will help to create a weekend environment that would make an invitation to the White House pale in comparison.

◆ **Weekend checklist**

Guest Bedrooms • A proper guest bedroom should contain:

Fresh linens on a beautifully made bed

Extra blankets and pillows

Television

Radio

Fresh flowers

A bowl of fruit, a fruit knife and napkins

An assortment of juices and bottled water

A small box of chocolates

An assortment of magazines and books

Adequate space in closets and drawers

A sufficient supply of hangers (include skirt, trouser and coat hangers)

A scented candle and a book of matches

A reading lamp

An alarm clock

Guest Bathrooms • Guest bathrooms should be scrupulously cleaned and stocked with supplies before your guests arrive (see "Bathrooms"). A proper guest bathroom should include:

Freshly laundered hand, face and bath towels

Fresh flowers

Soap

Shampoo and conditioner

Hair dryer

Shower cap

Perfume and cologne

Mouthwash

Bubble bath, bath salts and oils

Toothbrush and toothpaste

Disposable razor and shaving cream

Sanitary napkins

Condoms

Sewing kit

Sun tan creams and lotions

A humidifier in the winter

Meal Preparation • For menu planning:

1. Plan ahead: Don't wait until your guests have arrived before deciding what to make for dinner. Although you may favor the special joys of spontaneity, last-minute meal-planning might make your guests nervous. If possible, shop for the weekend ahead of time.

2. Don't plan menus that require endless preparation: The point of inviting weekend guests is to spend time with them—not with your pots and pans. You may want to include some of your willing guests in meal preparation. I have often found that "kitchen conversation" can be quite intimate. Meal *preparation can also be an excellent opportunity for getting to know someone better.*

3. Breakfast? Lunch? Dinner? *I offer weekend visitors simple yet elegant luncheons and dinners but tell them to "help themselves" for breakfast. Before retiring for the evening I prepare the coffee machine and place an assortment of breakfast cereals, teas, muffins (in a glass covered container), plates, glasses, etc. on the kitchen counter. I find that a scheduled sit-down breakfast is too constricting for weekend visitors. Some people like to rise with the sun; others feel that Saturdays do not begin before 10 A.M. A self-service buffet lets your guests set their own clocks.*

House Rules • Either formally or informally communicated, house rules establish behavioral and procedural guidelines. While the idea of "rules" may sound confining, the "dos and don'ts of domestic comingling" will help your guests to relax by answering unspoken (yet often contemplated) questions.

> **Meals:** *Decide upon an approach for serving breakfast, lunch and dinner; let your guests know the schedule. Based upon who you invite (and the circumstances) you may request assistance with setting the table and clearing and washing the dishes. I always prefer setting the table myself because I enjoy creating a picture-perfect table (see "Setting the Table"). When entertaining weekend guests I often accept offers of assistance in clearing and washing the dishes.*

183

Bedrooms: *Unless you specifically instruct them not to, guests should assume responsibility for keeping their rooms tidy and making their own beds.*

Schedules: *If you have special events planned for the weekend (theatre tickets, attending a party at someone else's home) let your guests know as soon as possible. If the social schedule requires specific wardrobe considerations, let them know in advance.*

Pools (if applicable): *If you do not want your guests to have access to the pool 24 hours a day let them know. Tell them that for their safety and to ensure the privacy of everyone in the house you prefer that no one swims past midnight (or whatever time you choose).*

◆ **Reminders**

1. Keep house rules simple and to the point. You don't want your guests to feel as if they've been invited to reform school. Don't bombard them with a set of rules as soon as they arrive: relate the necessary information as the occasion arises.

2. Air out guest rooms as far in advance as possible.

3. Don't feel as if you have to entertain your guests non-stop. Encourage them to go for a walk, a bicycle ride or a drive if they so desire. Allow them (and yourself) the freedom to enjoy some independent activity. Remember: they're your guests—not your prisoners.

◆ If you're the weekend guest

1. If your weekend hosts have a maid or housekeeper it is considered good manners to leave a tip. Depending on the length of the visit and the attentiveness of the staff member, $20–$50 would be polite.

2. Remember that "It is more blessed to give than to receive." Take a gift. Suitable offerings include: a bottle of champagne or wine; fresh or homemade breads, muffins, pies and cookies; smoked salmon; gourmet jams and jellies; cookbooks; chocolates.

Wine

You don't have to be an expert, take a class at the local college or read an assortment of books to feel confident about selecting and serving wine. You do have to be willing to ask questions, experiment and take risks. The best wines are often the ones you stumble across by accident in your local wine shop. The liquor store in my Greenwich Village neighborhood is packed so full of merchandise I'm constantly bumping into shelves, trying to dodge customers. One day I "bumped" into a lovely (and inexpensive) California Chardonnay that I then purchased for lack of a better inspiration; I have been drinking it ever since. Don't be intimidated by the endless selection of wines. If you're in a restaurant or bar, attending a wedding reception or visiting a friend's home and you sample a wine you like—ask questions, find the name and try it out the next time you entertain.

For those of you who have never made your own, wine is created through a fermentation process that involves combining grapes, sugar, and yeast. The process is complete when all of the sugar has been converted into alcohol or, in the case of certain sweet wines (sauternes), the alcohol level has reached 15 percent. Although the most popular wines originate in France, the United States

> **"Wine can of their wits the wise beguile**
> **Make the sage frolic and the serious smile."**
>
> **—Homer's "The Odyssey"**

(New York, California and Washington primarily), and Italy, there are some perfectly acceptable (and inexpensive) wines that are produced in Spain, Portugal, Germany and Australia.

◆ Types of wine

The following is a list of the three most popular types of red and white wines. It is by no means exhaustive but should be used as a "jumping-off point." When selecting a wine, your choice will be influenced by such characteristics as light or heavy bodied, dry or sweet, particular regions of origin (as you become more proficient) and, of course, price.

RED

- Cabernet Sauvignon: *This grape is used to create some of the greatest red wines in the world. Grown in both France and California, cabernet sauvignon is characterized by its dry, full-bodied taste.*

- Beaujolais: *One of the most popular red wines, beaujolais is known for its light, fruity taste and inexpensive price tag. Each November liquor stores around the world stock up with "beaujolais nouveau," a wine which is quickly created and meant to be quickly consumed.*

- Chianti: *This popular Italian red wine from the Tuscany region of Italy usually conjures images of* red-and-white checkered table cloths and spaghetti dinners. Most consumers do not realize that Chianti is actually a combination of red and white grapes.

WHITE

- Chablis: Chablis is a French province in the northernmost region in Burgundy that produces only white wine; although the name "Chablis" is frequently used to indicate "white wine," only wine made from grapes grown in the Chablis district is true Chablis.

- Chardonnay: Most of the finest white wines are made from the green-skinned Chardonnay grape which is grown in both France and California. Chardonnay is sometimes aged in oak barrels which gives it a slightly woody taste.

- Riesling: This white grape grown in France, California and Germany is used to produce an inexpensive dry white wine.

Brand Name	Average Price Per Bottle
Red	
Beaujolais Nouveau (French)	$6–$8
Zinfandel (California)	$8–$10
Merlot (New York State)	$8–$10
Mouton-Cadet (French)	$10–$12
Cabernet Sauvignon (California)	$10–$20
Pinot Noir (California)	$12–$25

Chianti Classico (Italian)	$12–$15
Châteauneuf-du-Pape (French)	$20–$30
Château Beychevelle (French)	$25–$30
Château Margaux (French)	$50–$100

White

Soave (Italian)	$8–$10
Fumé Blanc (California)	$10–$12
Pino Grigio (Italian)	$10–$12
Gavi (Italian)	$10–$12
Chardonnay (Australia)	$10–$12
Mouton-Cadet (French)	$10–$12
Chardonnay (California)	$15–$20
Sancerre (French)	$15–$20
Pouilly Fuissé (French)	$18–$22
Pouilly Fumé (French)	$18–$22
Château d'Yquem (a dessert wine)	$125–$200

◆ Chilling wine

Chilling wines is a matter of personal taste. Most people prefer white wine chilled, red wine at room temperature. An inexpensive red wine, however, can certainly be improved by a few hours of "aging" in the refrigerator. If you decide to chill wine, always use a wine cooler once the bottle has been opened to maintain the temperature.

◆ Important considerations when serving wine

Glasses • Wine glasses are available in a wide range of styles and shapes. Based upon your taste and budget a single glass can cost a few dollars or several hundred for a piece of Bacarat or Lalique crystal. No matter the budget, I recommend the use of clear (not colored or tinted) wine glasses which are not intricately etched or carved. Part of the wine drinking experience is being able to see the color through the glass, watching the graceful movement of the magnificent liquid as you swirl it around with a professional flick of the wrist. The rich, red shade of a bordeaux or burgundy adds a wonderful splash of color to a beautifully set table.

The ideal size for most wine glasses is between 12–14 ounces. I prefer the drama of oversized (18–22 ounce) glasses but only use them on occasion: guests sometimes find the large size awkward to drink from. Recently I entertained a few friends; when one of the female guests couldn't quite maneuver the colossal crystal, she ended up dribbling a very fine Merlot down the front of her white satin blouse. Be wary of unusual shapes that may be interesting to look at but impractical to use. Unless you have the budget and storage capacity for multiple sets, purchase traditional wine glasses that are balloon shaped and curve inward at the top. They help to concentrate the bouquet and maintain the temperature of certain wines. A glass which is rounded inward at the top helps to retain the chill of a white wine; larger, balloon-shaped glasses allow maximum swirling for red wine.

Uncorking • Many hosts are as traumatized by the thought of uncorking wine as they are about opening a bottle of champagne. Like any skill, it requires patience and practice—*and* a good corkscrew. But with the endless varieties of corkscrews currently available on the market choosing the "perfect" one can be as perplexing as selecting wine. I prefer the stainless steel model that is popular in bars and available in most supermarkets. Resembling a metallic extraterrestrial, this particular model features a bottle opener ("head") on one end, a corkscrew on the other, with prong-like "arms" on either side. As the screw is inserted into the cork by twisting the head, the arms elevate. Once the screw is firmly in place, gently push down on the arms to remove the cork. The most attractive feature of this particular corkscrew is that it can be used on a counter top. The perfect corkscrew is the one which is the easiest for *you* to manipulate. Experiment with the various types (in either your friends' homes or stores) before making a purchase.

If you accidentally break the cork or it appears to be stuck, don't panic or toss the bottle aside. Gently push the cork into the bottle with a screwdriver. Work slowly and carefully so that you don't hurt yourself. Once the cork is released into the bottle, strain the wine through a very fine sieve to remove the bits of cork.

People frequently wonder whether red wines need to be opened 20–30 minutes before serving to allow them to "breathe" properly. Although it certainly doesn't do any harm and adds some fun to the wine-drinking experience, I have rarely noticed a difference in taste. Unless I am pressed for time, however, I do allow red wines to breathe: why risk offending the Gods of the Grape?

Pouring • When serving wine in your home, it isn't necessary to go through the ritual of examining and sniffing the cork and tasting the wine. Of course, if you want to have a little fun, designate one of your guests the wine expert for the evening; allow him or her to "pass judgment." To allow for maximum swirling (which is half the fun of drinking wine) never fill a wine glass more than half full.

◆ Matching wine with food

Unlike federal laws or the ten commandments, the rhyming rules of gastronomical delights are not printed in official books or set in stone: they're guidelines that are meant to be broken. If you're serving steak and happen to be a white wine enthusiast, the FAD ("Food and Drink") Police won't knock down your front door and carry you away. Make choices that appeal to your own tastes. Light and subtle wines (usually white) are compatible with such light meals as chicken and fish because the delicate flavors enhance each other. The robust tastes of full-bodied wines (usually red) are normally served with stews, casseroles, and beef, lamb and pork dishes, whose hearty flavors will not be overpowered. When in doubt, however, trust your own palette.

◆ 4 reasons for serving wine

Combines Well with Food • A carefully selected wine (unlike hard liquor) will enhance the flavor of fine food. It is disheartening to spend hours in the kitchen only to have subtle flavors masked by scotch and sodas during the meal.

> "With fish, serve white
> With meat serve red
> If not, I fear
> You'll be shot dead."
> —Anonymous

Cost-Effective • You can save money by serving wine instead of stocking the bar with liquor, juice, and soda. A case of Beaujolais Nouveau (12 bottles) can be purchased for $70 and will last for 3 to 4 small dinner parties.

Time-Saving • As with champagne, serving wine exclusively allows you to spend more time with your guests; it simplifies the often complicated process of mixing, garnishing, serving, and remaking individual cocktails.

Easier to Monitor Guests' Alcohol Consumption • Monitoring the alcohol level of your guests is easier if you serve only wine. Keep track of how many bottles you've served and in what amount of time.